HIDDEN HEARTBREAK

HI! IS NOW AN OK TIME TO STOP BY?

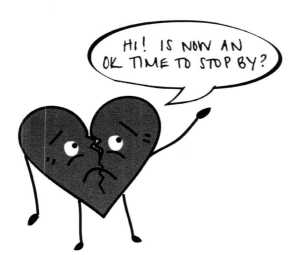

Andrews McMeel Publishing
a division of Andrews McMeel Universal
1130 Walnut Street, Kansas City, Missouri 64106

www.andrewsmcmeel.com

www.instagram.com/hiddenheartbreak

18 19 20 21 22 SDB 10 9 8 7 6 5 4 3 2 1

ISBN: 978-1-4494-9483-4

Library of Congress Control Number: 2018945141

Editor: Allison Adler
Art Director/Designer: Julie Barnes
Production Editor: Margaret Utz
Production Manager: Carol Coe

ATTENTION: SCHOOLS AND BUSINESSES
Andrews McMeel books are available at quantity discounts with bulk purchase for educational, business, or sales promotional use. For information, please e-mail the Andrews McMeel Publishing Special Sales Department: specialsales@amuniversal.com.

TO MY PARENTS,
FOR TEACHING ME RESILIENCE;
TO MY FAMILY AND FRIENDS; AND TO EVERYONE
WHO HAS EVER NURSED A BROKEN HEART,
INCLUDING YOU, BIRDSHIRT

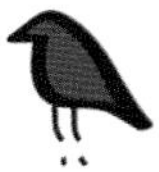

IT'S HAPPENED TO ALL OF US: You encounter someone and feel a powerful connection. Maybe it's someone you've had a weakness for your whole life, or maybe it's someone you're meeting for the very first time. Colors look brighter; your face is permanently plastered with a smile; your heart is on fire every minute of the day.

Maybe this feeling lasts for a few weeks, months, or even years. You remain euphoric, giddily floating through love songs, savoring every note and word, convinced that you have found The One. And then, out of nowhere, the record screeches to a halt: The One doesn't feel the same way. They feel stifled and need to focus on themselves. They have emotional walls that can't be broken down. They love you but they're not "in love" with you.

How could that be possible? Didn't they say there was magic between the two of you? Didn't they love discussing art, music, and writing with you? Weren't they just telling you about that vacation they wanted to take together six months from now?

I've been there—more than once—and I'm here to help. My art therapy journey began when the man I thought was

the love of my life confessed that he couldn't love me. Much
as a writer might use a journal to process their emotions,
I decided to use the medium I knew best—drawing—to
deal with my grief and humiliation. Through introspection,
acceptance, and most importantly, laughter, I hoped my art
would help me move on.

But what began as a solitary journey soon became something
much more. One day, partially out of a thirst for empathy
and, let's be honest, partially out of spite, I posted a few of
my drawings on Instagram. The response was immediate,
and my few little drawings quickly turned into hundreds of
vulnerable, emotional, and sometimes cringe-worthy cartoons
that resonated with thousands of people. Everyone has had
their heart broken; what better medicine is there than
to connect with others who are experiencing the same
misfortune?

I hope my comics will make you laugh, cry, and emphatically
think, "Me too!" I hope I can show you that beyond empathy,
humor, and time, the best medicine for a broken heart is a
reminder of your resilience, strength, and ability to rise. But
most importantly, I hope my art will help you heal, the way
creating this art helped heal me.

THE COURTSHIP: THE INITIAL SPARK IS IRRESISTIBLE

It starts off innocently, and perhaps that's part of the draw. The first touch, a shared giggle, an out-of-the-blue Instagram like. Something inside of your heart awakens, and you suddenly can't remember what it felt like to make it through a day without that exhilarating, intoxicating feeling—the initial rush of infatuation, from a magnetic conversation to the dizziness of a first kiss. I've always been one to follow my heart, and oh, the places my heart has taken me!

HIM!

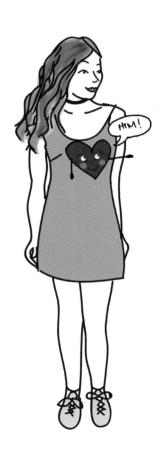

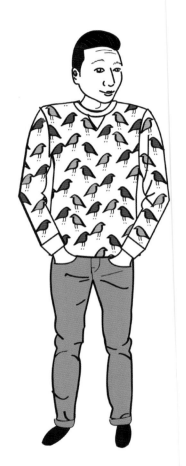

if you say so.

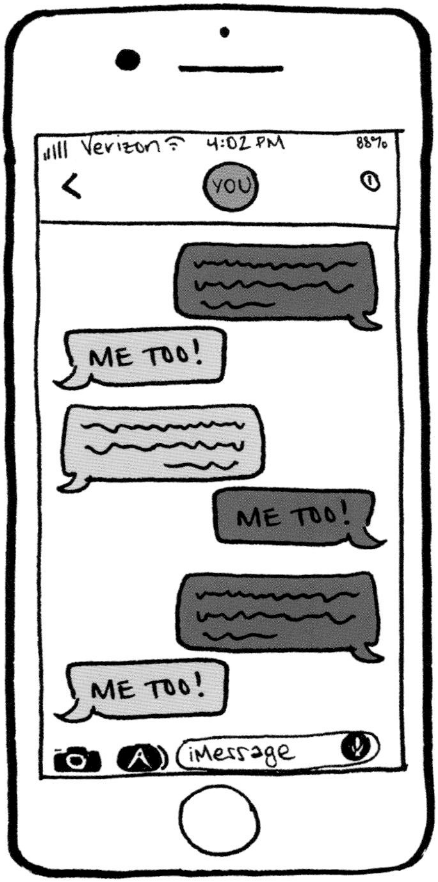
Verizon 4:02 PM 88%
YOU
ME TOO!
ME TOO!
ME TOO!
iMessage

that addictive ping-pong match.

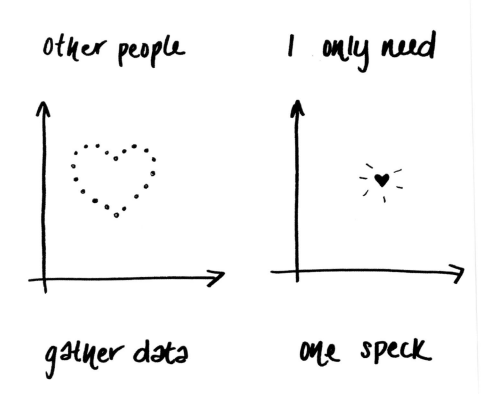

other people

gather data

I only need

one speck

I don't analyze, I idealize.

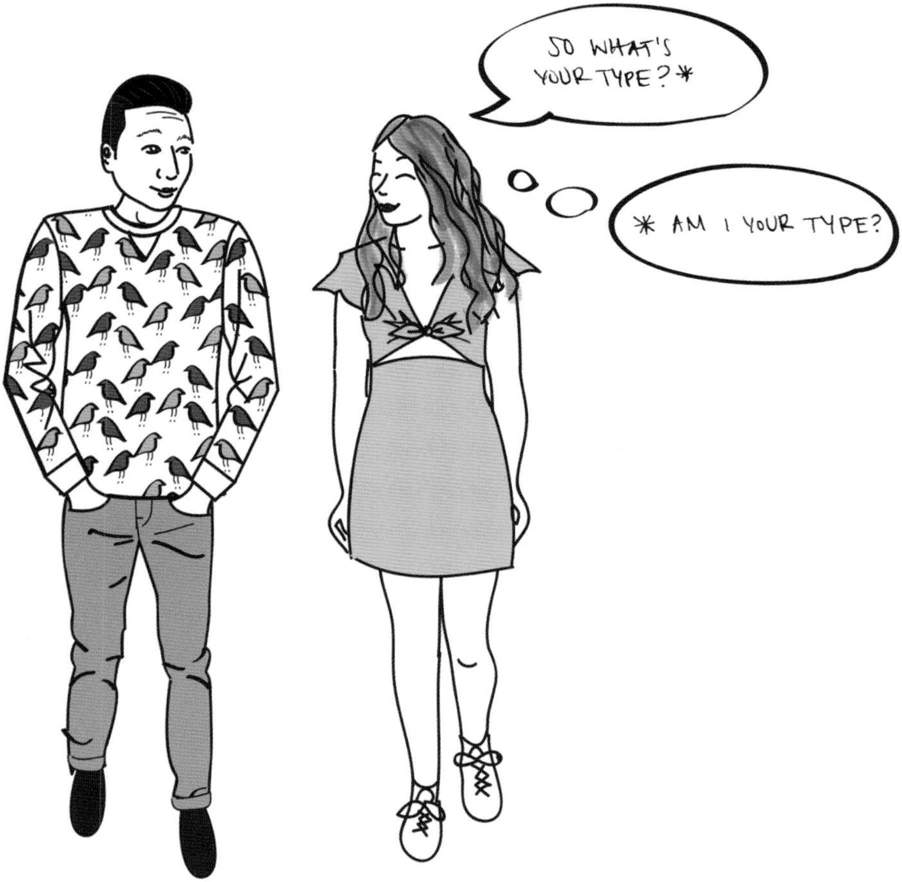
SO WHAT'S YOUR TYPE? *
* AM I YOUR TYPE?

a very loaded question.

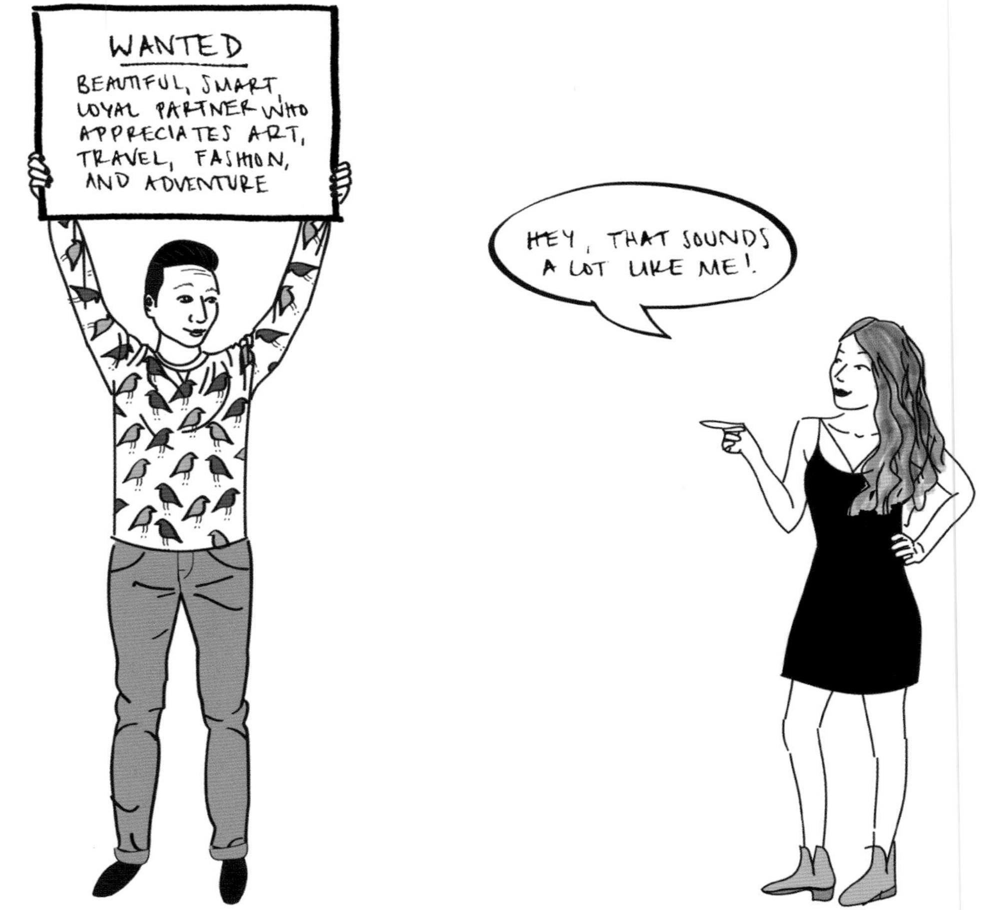
WANTED
BEAUTIFUL, SMART, LOYAL PARTNER WHO APPRECIATES ART, TRAVEL, FASHION, AND ADVENTURE
HEY, THAT SOUNDS A LOT LIKE ME!

I hope you offer good benefits.

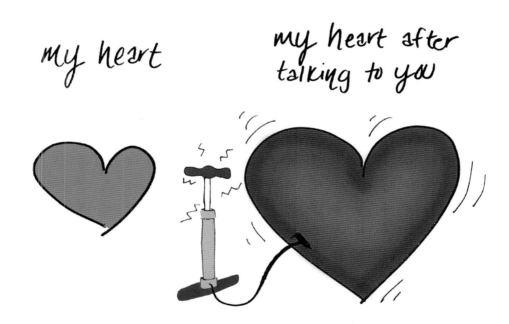

my heart

my heart after talking to you

pump it up.

I LOVE THE
WAY YOU WORK!

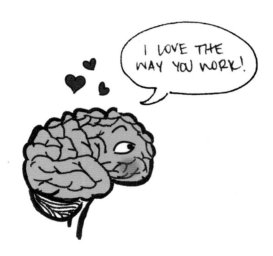

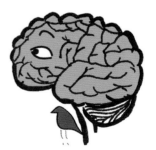

a chemical kind of art.

the feeling of you
looking at me

like everything I did
was magic

you always had a good eye.

our first kiss

HOW I REMEMBER IT:

HOW IT REALLY WAS:

EYES WIDE OPEN FROM SHOCK OF SO MUCH TONGUE

LITERALLY SWALLOWING ME WHOLE

FRIZZY FROM CAR RIDE

SUPER AWKWARD BACKPACK MY HANDS KEPT GETTING STUCK IN

SWEATY FROM CAR RIDE

but it was still perfect.

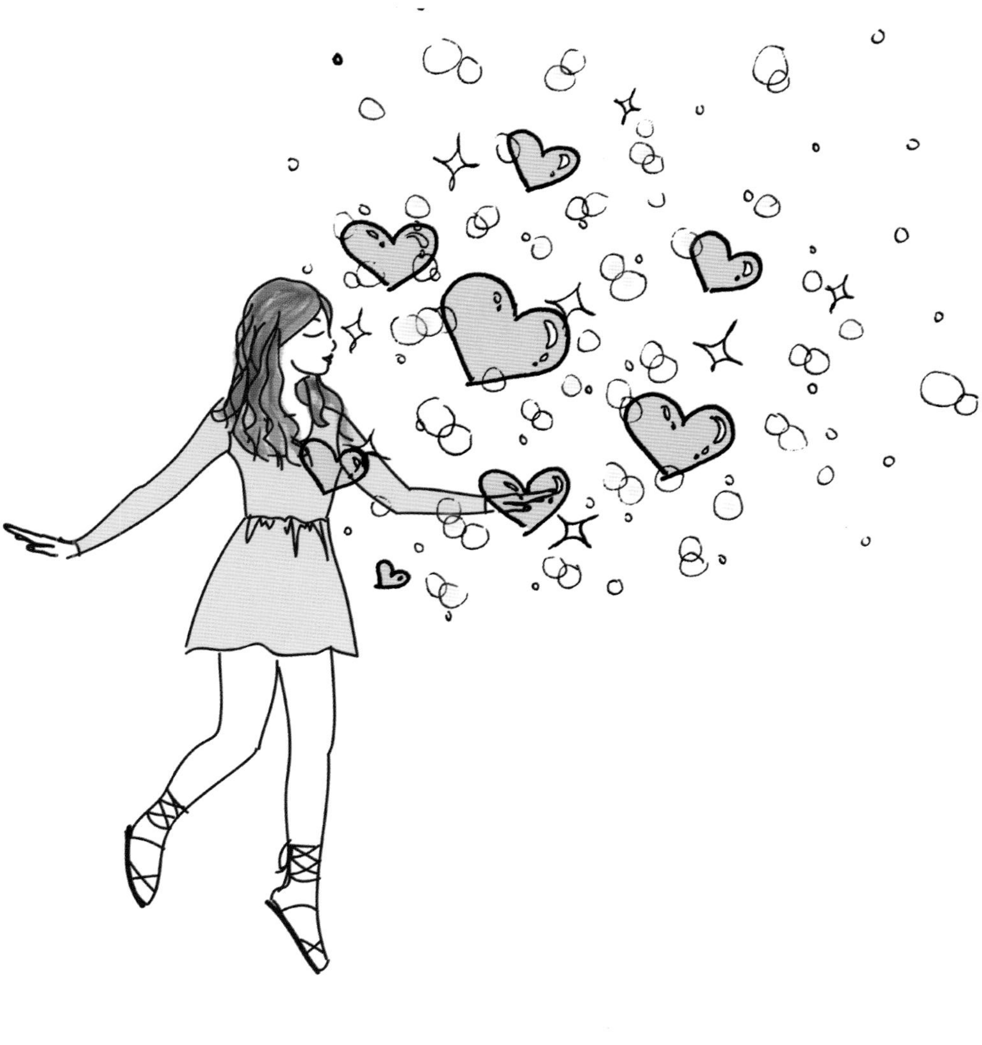

nothing can possibly go wrong.

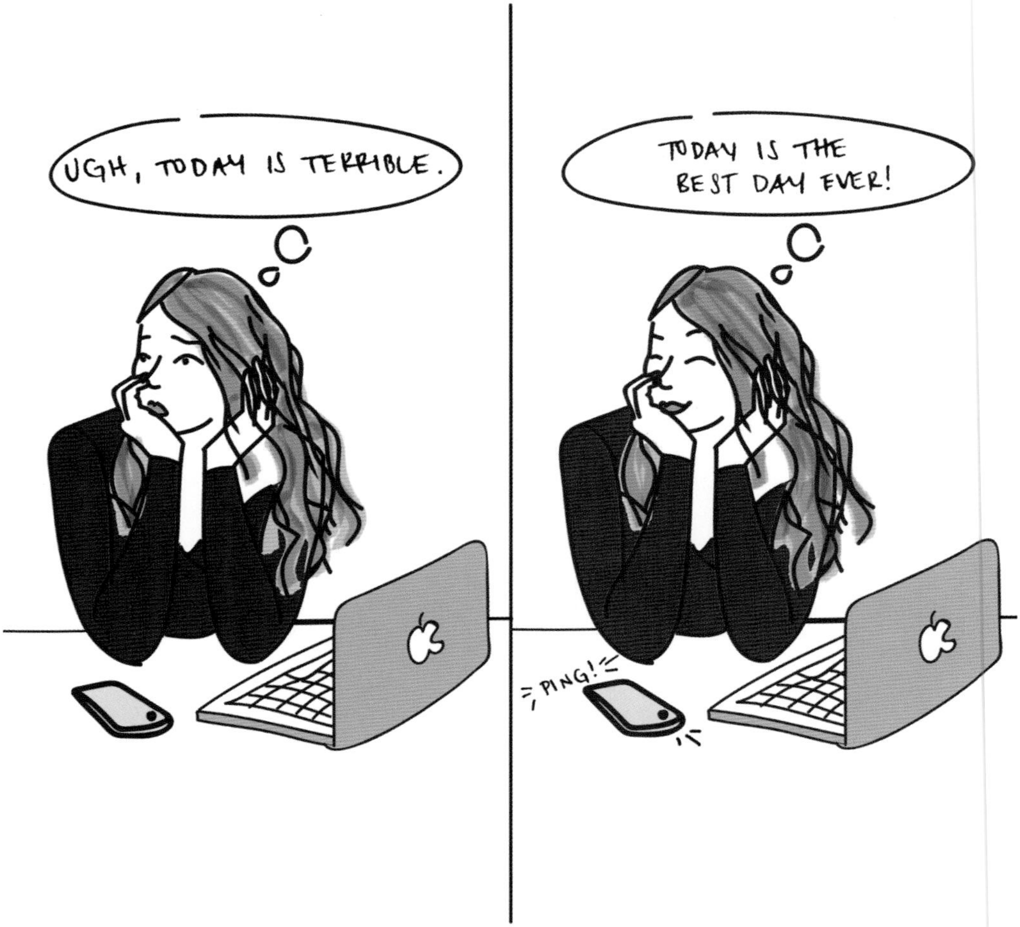
UGH, TODAY IS TERRIBLE.
TODAY IS THE BEST DAY EVER!
PING!

one little ping and my whole mood swings.

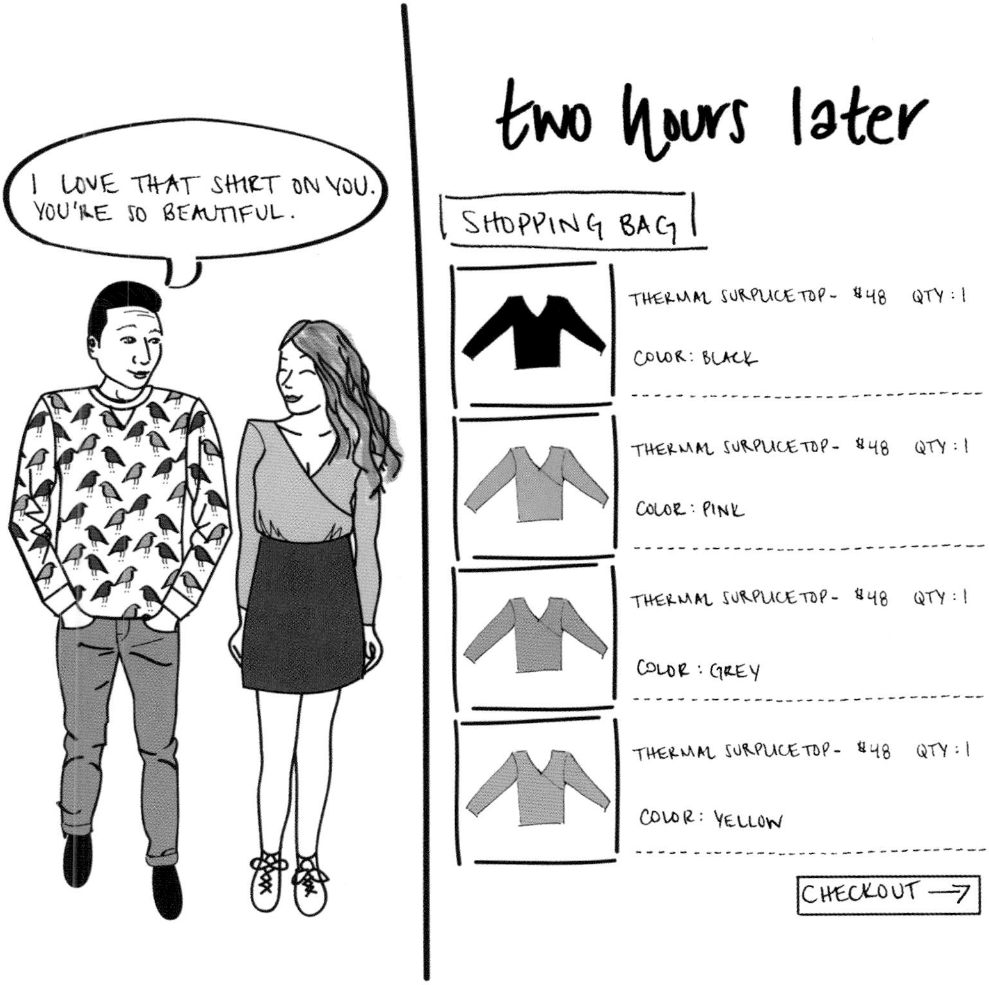
I LOVE THAT SHIRT ON YOU. YOU'RE SO BEAUTIFUL.
two hours later
SHOPPING BAG
THERMAL SURPLICE TOP - $48 QTY: 1
COLOR: BLACK
THERMAL SURPLICE TOP - $48 QTY: 1
COLOR: PINK
THERMAL SURPLICE TOP - $48 QTY: 1
COLOR: GREY
THERMAL SURPLICE TOP - $48 QTY: 1
COLOR: YELLOW
CHECKOUT

must. buy. every. color.

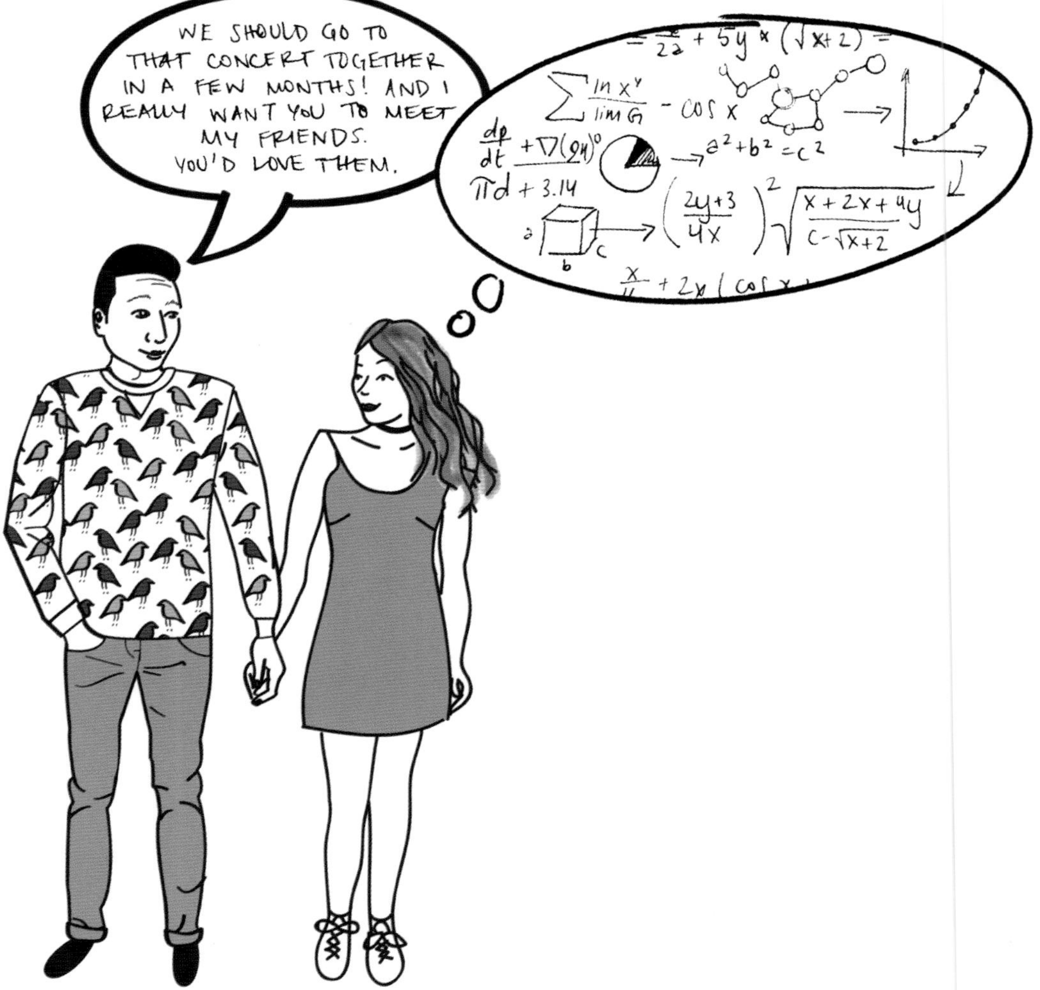
WE SHOULD GO TO THAT CONCERT TOGETHER IN A FEW MONTHS! AND I REALLY WANT YOU TO MEET MY FRIENDS. YOU'D LOVE THEM.
$a^2 + b^2 = c^2$
$\pi d + 3.14$
- COS X

what does it all mean?

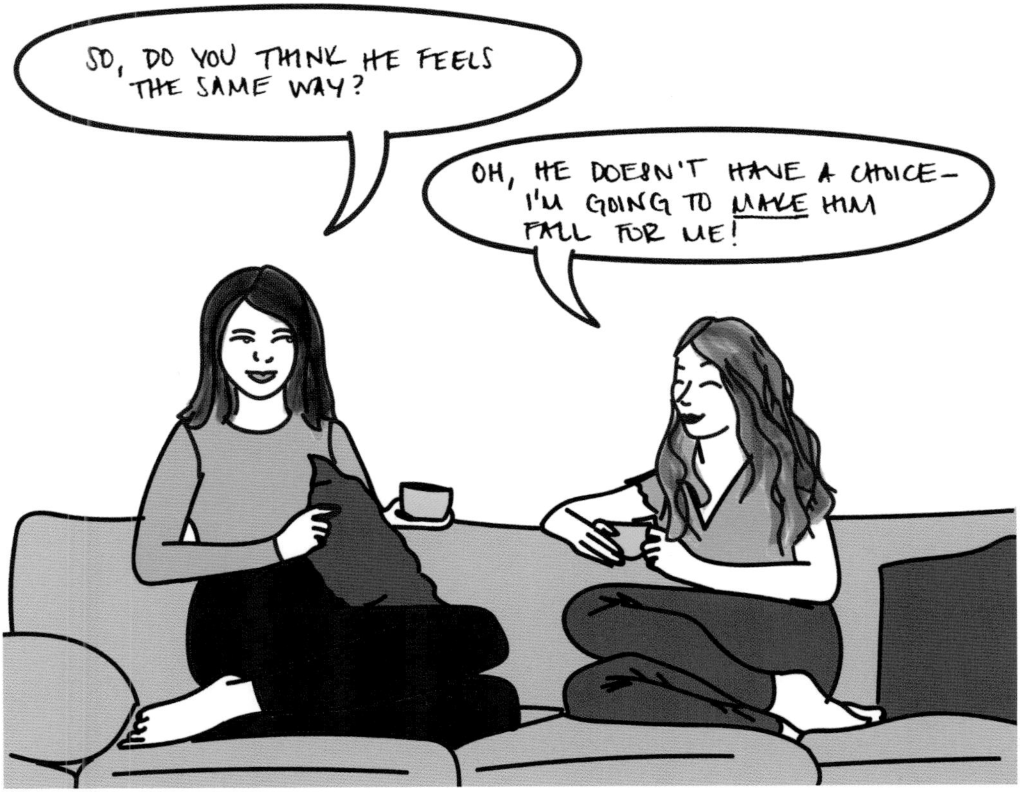
SO, DO YOU THINK HE FEELS THE SAME WAY?
OH, HE DOESN'T HAVE A CHOICE— I'M GOING TO MAKE HIM FALL FOR ME!

confident and stubborn—a winning combination.

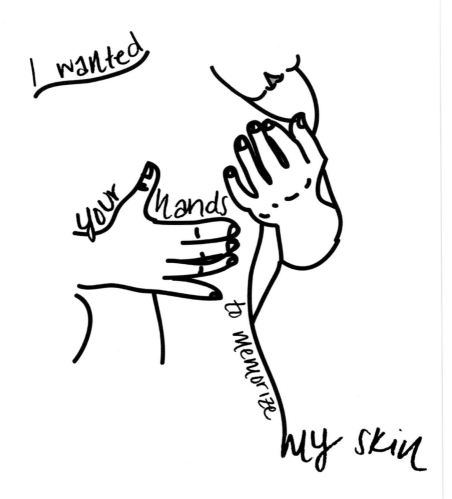

I wanted your hands to memorize my skin

worship every inch.

a cheap thrill

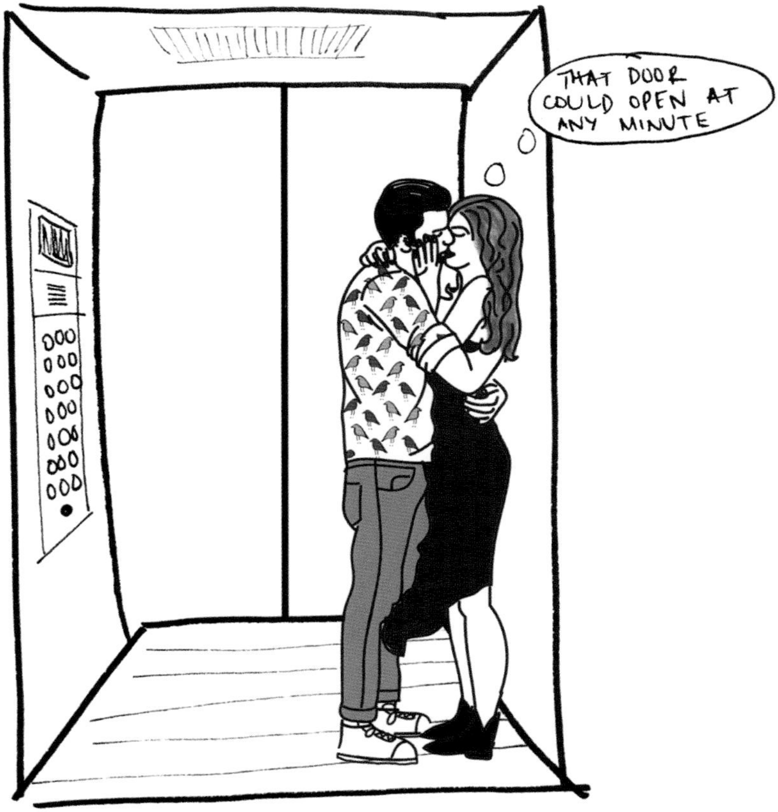
THAT DOOR COULD OPEN AT ANY MINUTE

I didn't need much with you.

HIS WAY OF MAKING ME FEEL SPECIAL WITH THE SMALLEST GESTURES

HIS PASSION FOR HIS CAREER

HIS INTELLECTUAL CURIOSITY

HIS CONFIDENCE

HIS APPRECIATION OF ART + MUSIC

HIS KINDNESS TOWARD OTHERS

a trick of the eye?

what hooked you?

a comparative study

HOW NORMAL PEOPLE FALL IN LOVE
OH! I LOVE YOU!
3 MONTHS
6 MONTHS
HOW I FALL IN LOVE
OMG! I LOVE YOU!
2 WEEKS

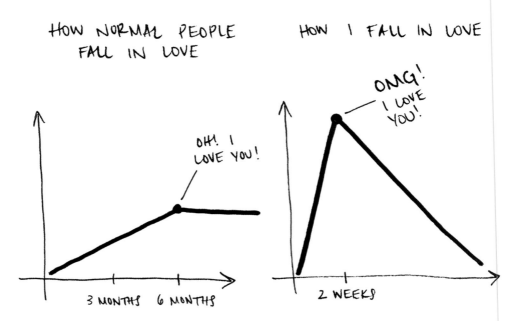

a lesson in instinct.

would you rather...

SLEEP	OR	SPEND TIME WITH THEM
GO TO THE GYM	or	SPEND TIME WITH THEM
EAT FOOD	OR	SPEND TIME WITH THEM
GO TO WORK	or	SPEND TIME WITH THEM
GO ON A VACATION	OR	SPEND TIME WITH THEM

these questions are all very rhetorical.

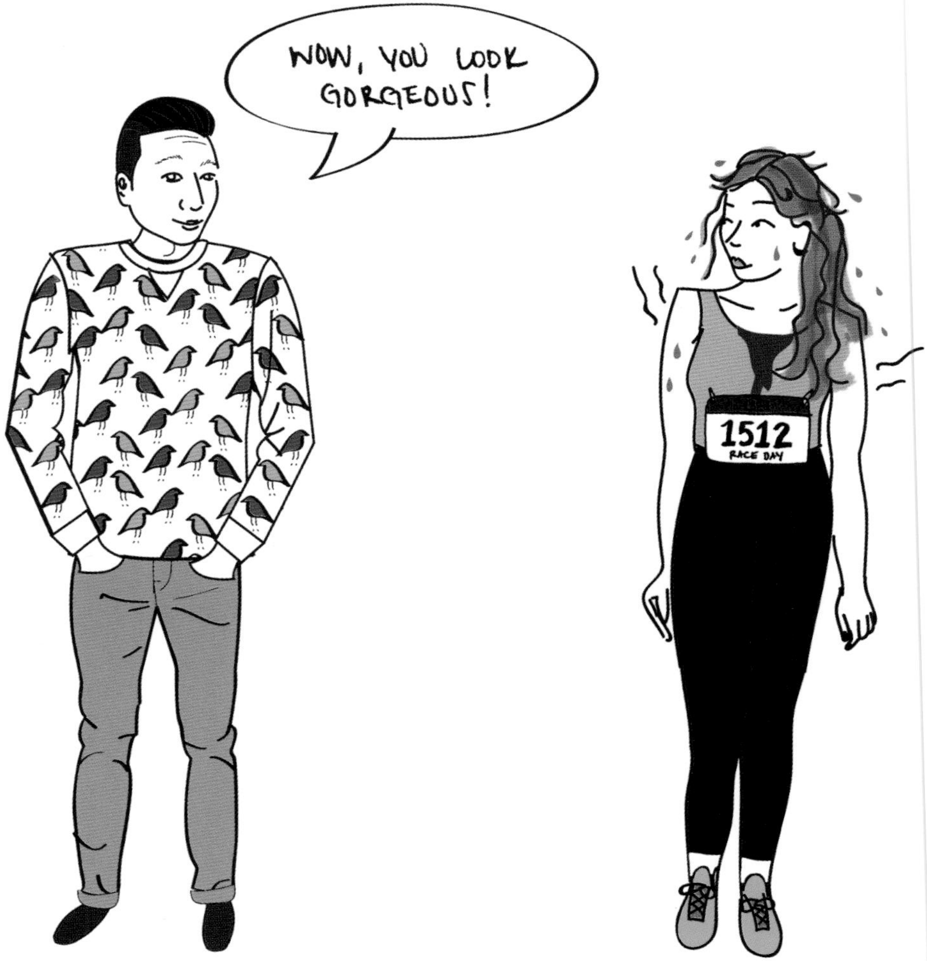
WOW, YOU LOOK GORGEOUS!
1512
RACE DAY

making sweat my signature scent.

me in love:
also me:
OMG I JUST FEEL LIKE I'M SO EXCITED ABOUT EVERYTHING, AND I WANT TO TELL YOU EVERY THOUGHT I HAVE AND SHARE SO MANY THINGS WITH YOU
OMG, DON'T SAY ANYTHING STUPID

a blessing and a curse.

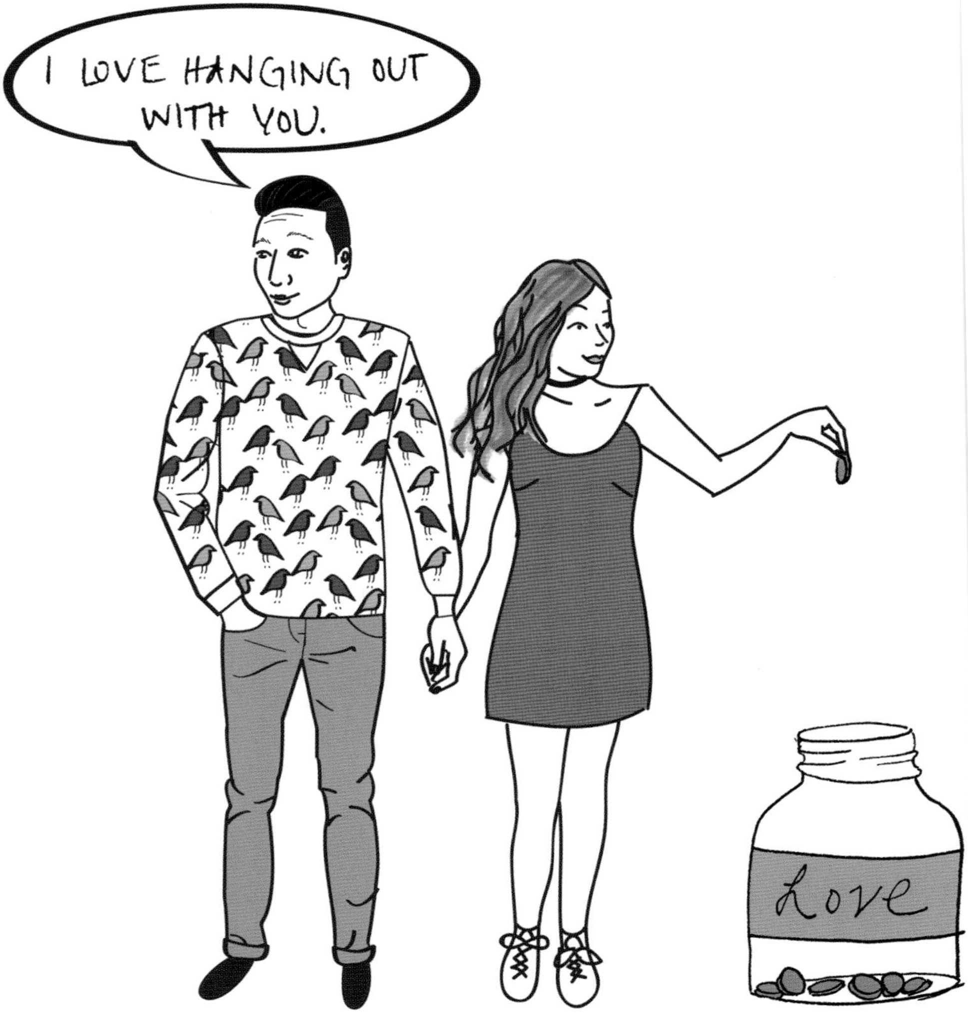
I LOVE HANGING OUT WITH YOU.
Love

just keeping a casual count.

BE WITH SOMEONE
WHO MAKES YOU FEEL

LIKE YOUR HEART
JUST GOT STAR POWER
IN MARIO KART

racing and glowing and rushing and overflowing.

HOOK, LINE, AND SINKER: YOU'RE ALREADY IN TOO DEEP

I'm an all-or-nothing kind of person. Pouring myself fully and openly into a relationship is the only way I know how to participate. With such passion often comes blindness, and in my case, a specific blindness to warning signs and red flags. From compliments that weren't really that meaningful to alarming pillow talk, I am an expert at ignoring it all. Sometimes you just have to laugh about the moments when your head was buried in the sand.

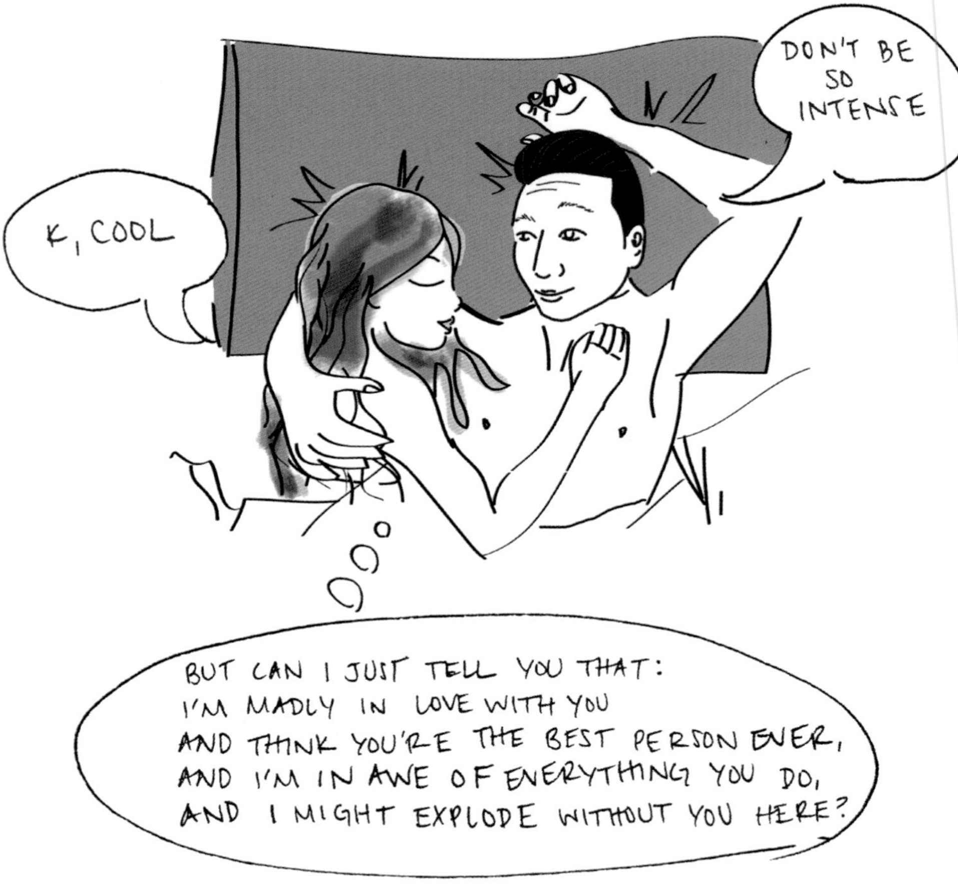
DON'T BE SO INTENSE
K, COOL
BUT CAN I JUST TELL YOU THAT:
I'M MADLY IN LOVE WITH YOU
AND THINK YOU'RE THE BEST PERSON EVER,
AND I'M IN AWE OF EVERYTHING YOU DO,
AND I MIGHT EXPLODE WITHOUT YOU HERE?

oops, I did it again.

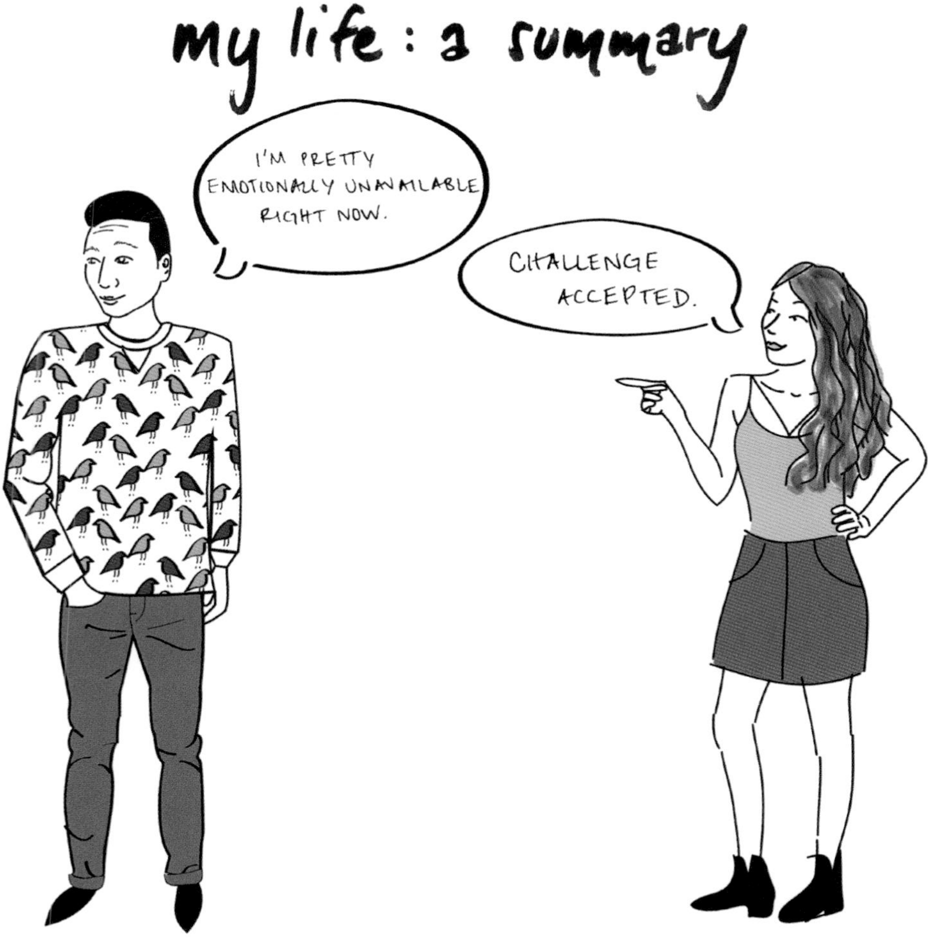
my life: a summary
I'M PRETTY EMOTIONALLY UNAVAILABLE RIGHT NOW.
CHALLENGE ACCEPTED.

I'm a glutton for punishment.

the statement	the objective	other acceptable outcomes
" I MISS YOU "	TO GET THEM TO SAY, "I MISS YOU TOO"	"I CAN'T WAIT TO SEE YOU AGAIN"
" WHAT ARE YOU UP TO TONIGHT? "	TO MAKE PLANS	A PHONE CALL UNTIL 2:00 AM
"DO YOU LIKE THIS OUTFIT?"	TO SOLICIT A COMPLIMENT	A SEDUCTION + REMOVAL OF SAID OUTFIT
"IS EVERYTHING OK?"	TO GET REASSURANCE	TO TALK THEM THROUGH WHATEVER IS BOTHERING THEM
"I'M HOPPING IN THE SHOWER, BRB"	TO MAKE THEM PICTURE YOU NAKED	THEY RUSH OVER TO JOIN YOU

all about the strategy.

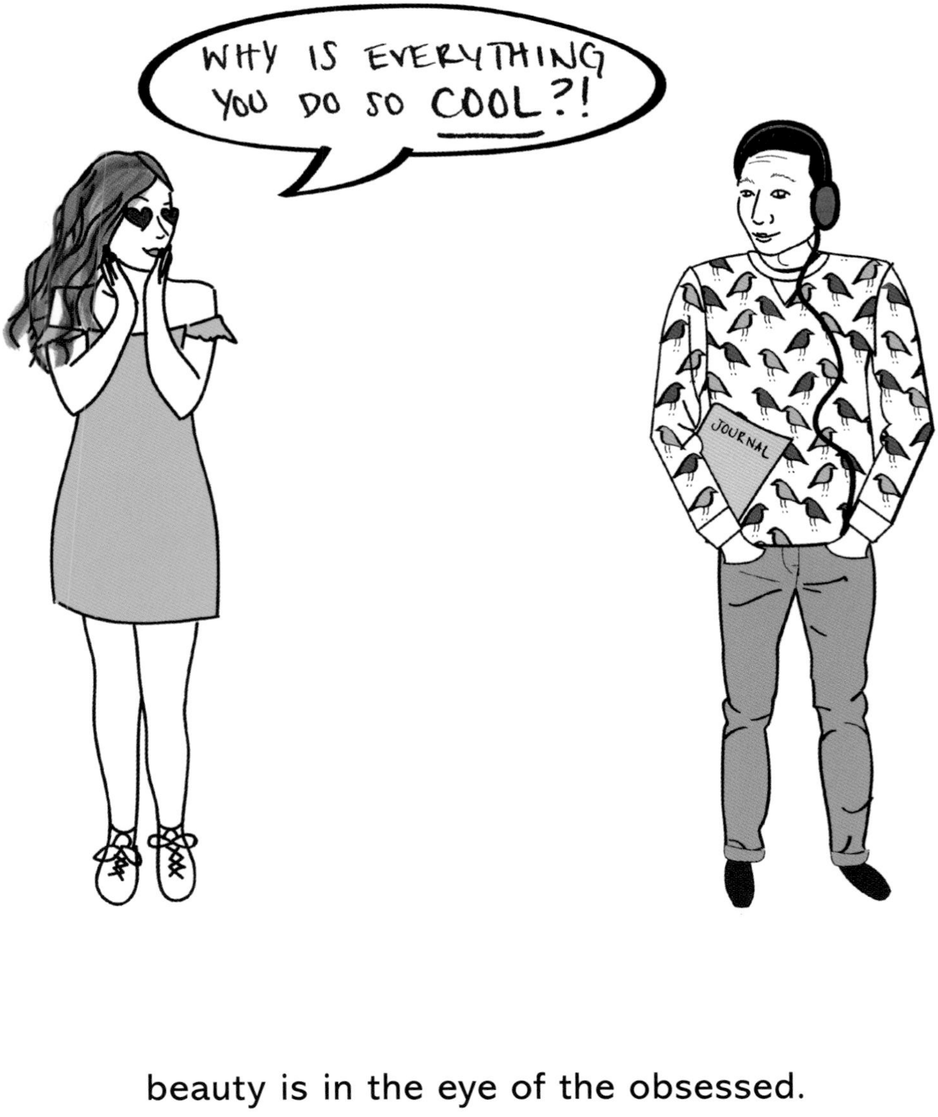
WHY IS EVERYTHING YOU DO SO COOL?!
JOURNAL

beauty is in the eye of the obsessed.

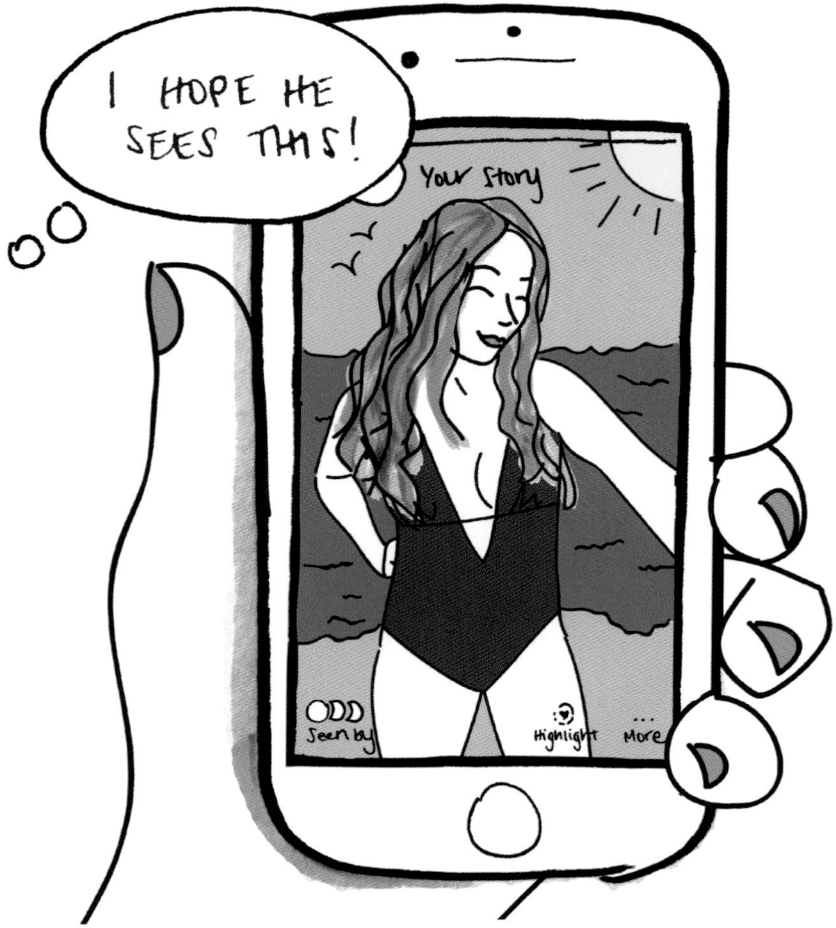
I HOPE HE SEES THIS!
Your Story
Seen by
Highlight
More

who else would I even post this for?

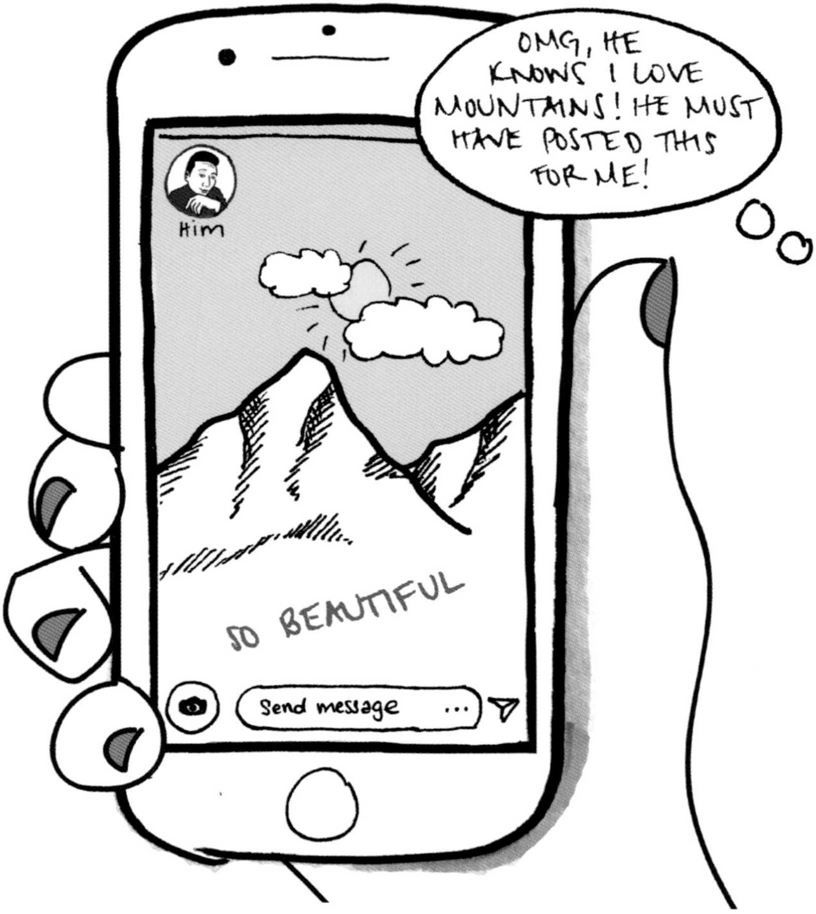
OMG, HE KNOWS I LOVE MOUNTAINS! HE MUST HAVE POSTED THIS FOR ME!
Him
SO BEAUTIFUL
Send message ...

who else would he even post this for?

things I won't do

PET A SNAKE

PERFORM IN A CABARET

CLIMB MT. EVEREST

DRINK STRAIGHT GIN

WEAR BODYCON DRESSES

BEE-KEEP

STAY OUT UNTIL 4:00AM

ATTEND AN IMPROV CLASS

RUN AN ULTRAMARATHON

things I'd be willing to do to spend time with him

PET A SNAKE

PERFORM IN A CABARET

CLIMB MT. EVEREST

DRINK STRAIGHT GIN

WEAR BODYCON DRESSES

BEE-KEEP

STAY OUT UNTIL 4:00AM

ATTEND AN IMPROV CLASS

RUN AN ULTRAMARATHON

boundaries? what are those?

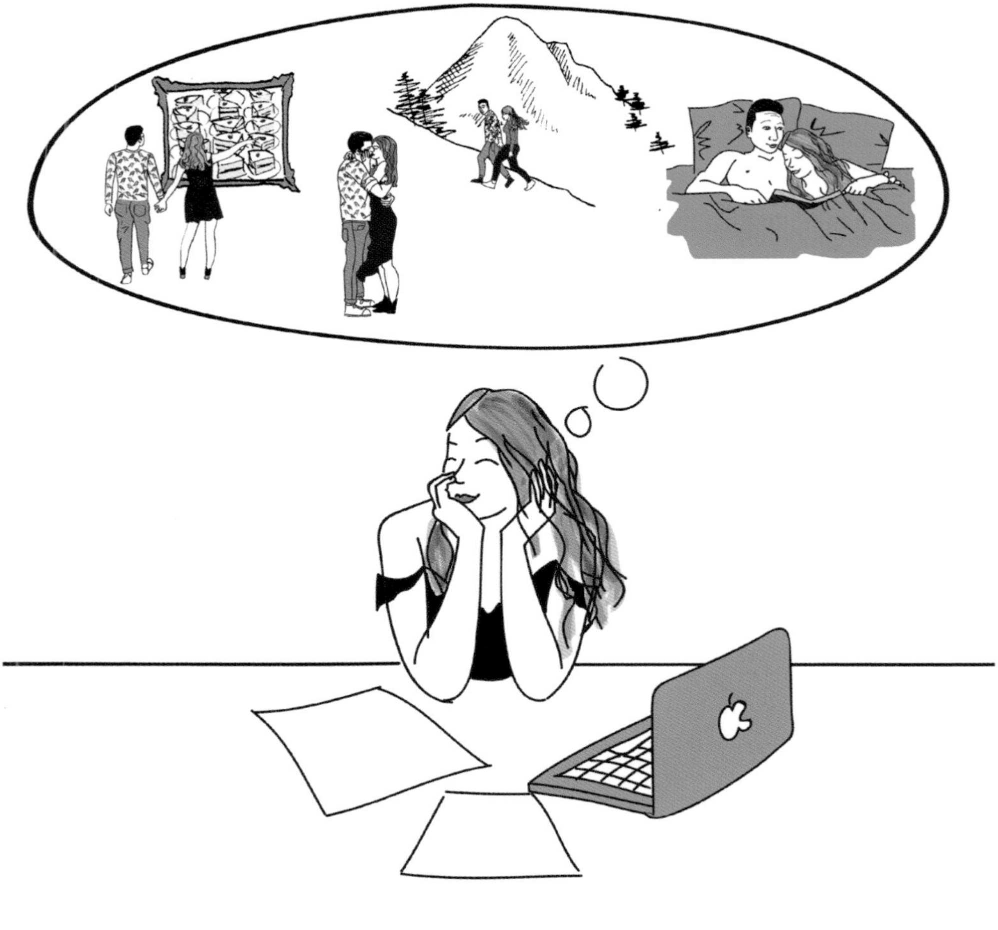

all of the things.

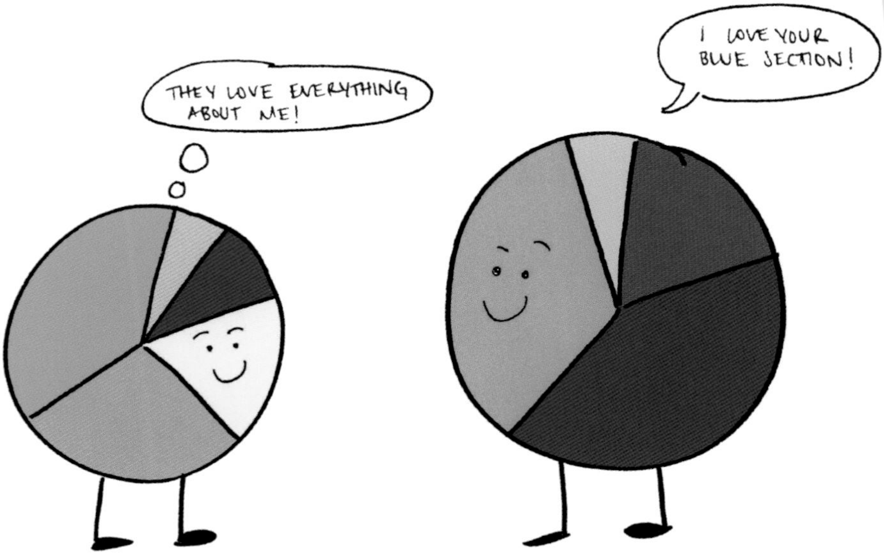
THEY LOVE EVERYTHING ABOUT ME!
I LOVE YOUR BLUE SECTION!

dangerous assumptions.

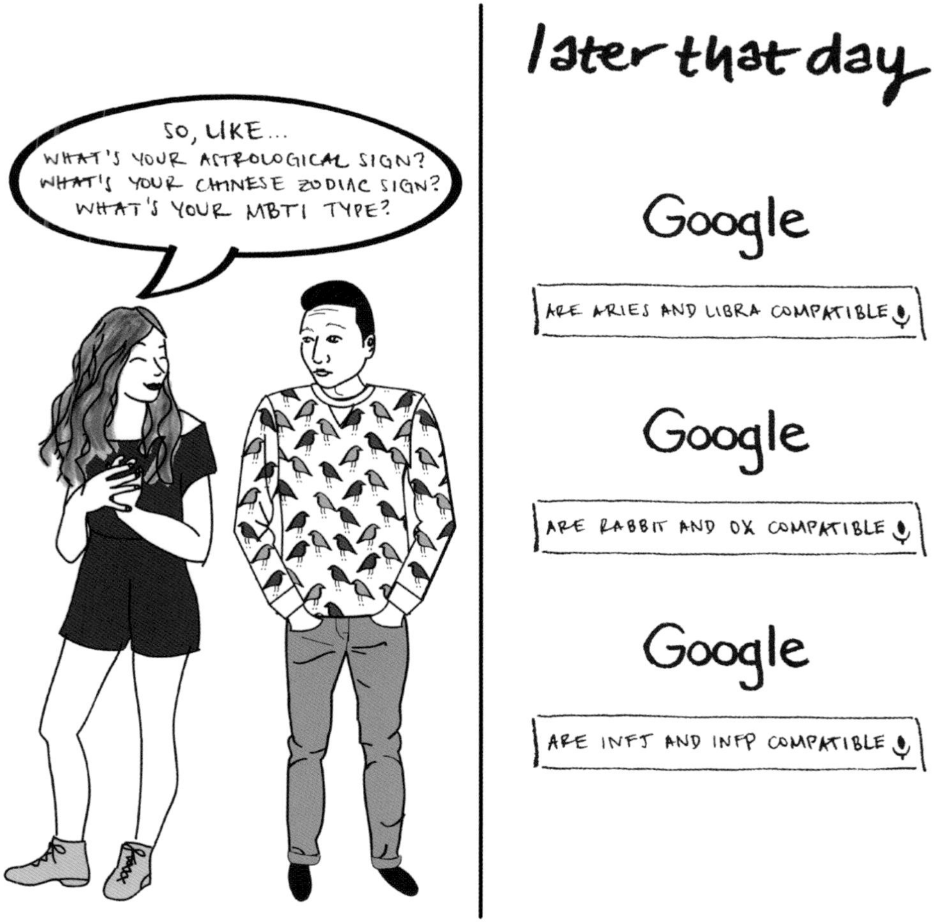
SO, LIKE...
WHAT'S YOUR ASTROLOGICAL SIGN?
WHAT'S YOUR CHINESE ZODIAC SIGN?
WHAT'S YOUR MBTI TYPE?
later that day
Google
ARE ARIES AND LIBRA COMPATIBLE
Google
ARE RABBIT AND OX COMPATIBLE
Google
ARE INFJ AND INFP COMPATIBLE

you can never be too well-informed.

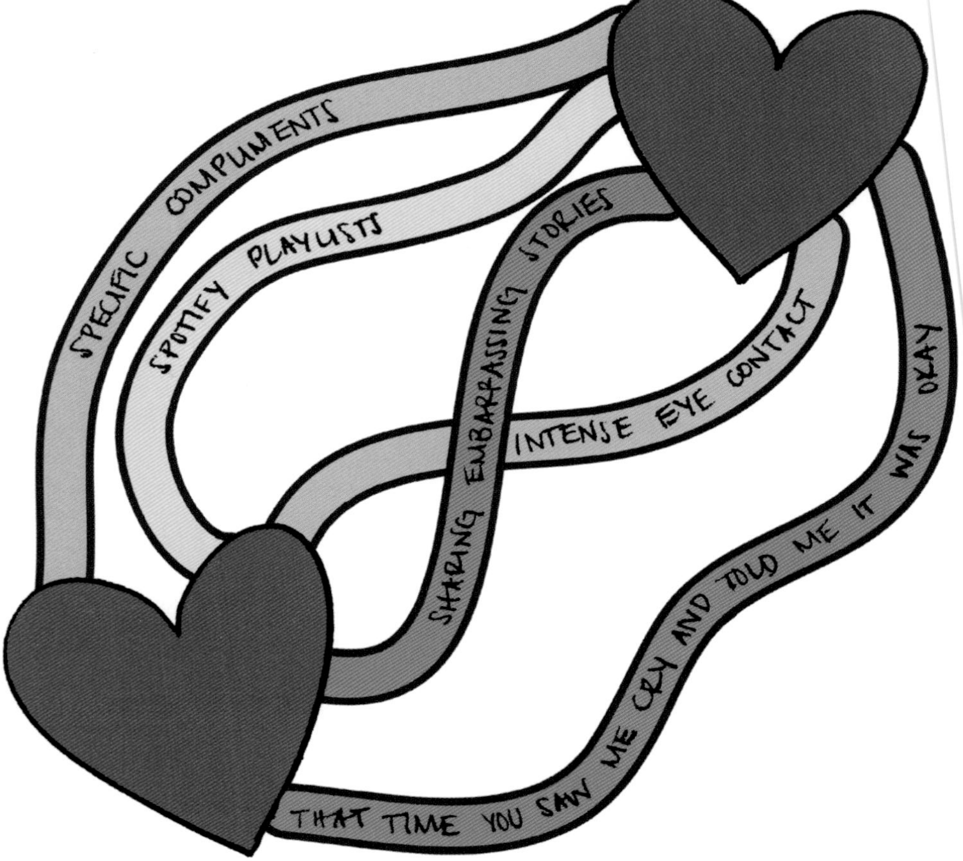
SPECIFIC COMPLIMENTS
SPOTIFY PLAYLISTS
SHARING EMBARRASSING STORIES
INTENSE EYE CONTACT
THAT TIME YOU SAW ME CRY AND TOLD ME IT WAS OKAY

latch on.

what made you feel connected?

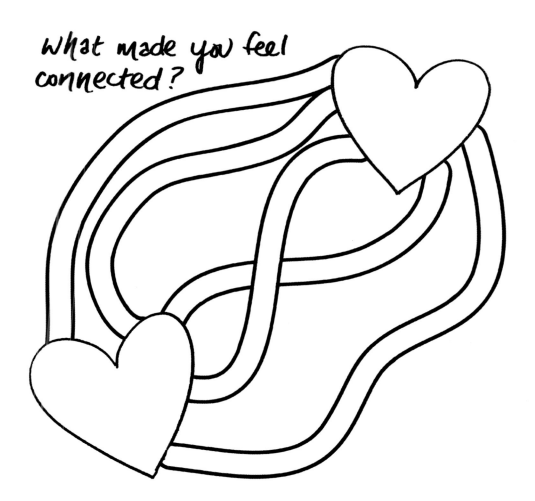

between the lines

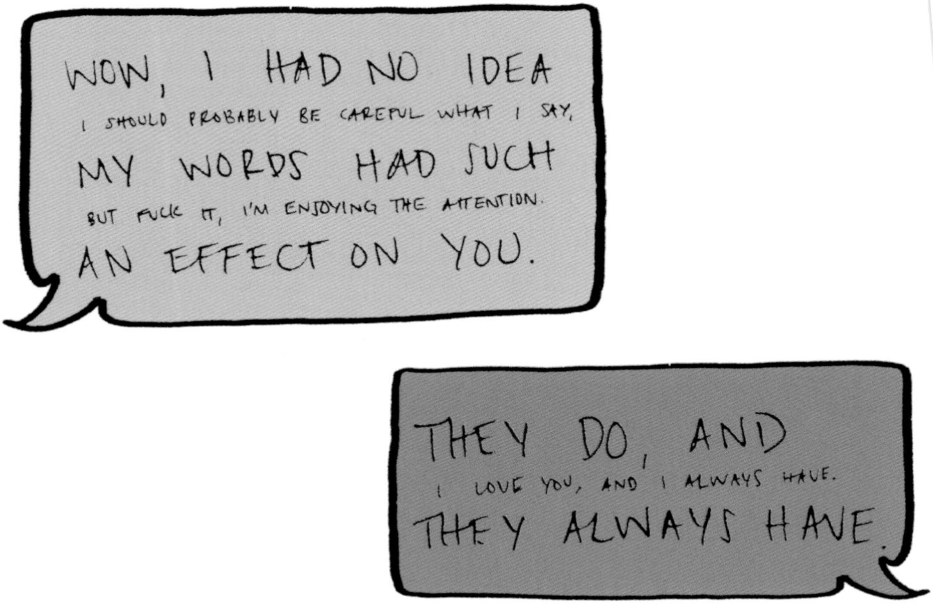
WOW, I HAD NO IDEA
I SHOULD PROBABLY BE CAREFUL WHAT I SAY,
MY WORDS HAD SUCH
BUT FUCK IT, I'M ENJOYING THE ATTENTION.
AN EFFECT ON YOU.
THEY DO, AND
I LOVE YOU, AND I ALWAYS HAVE.
THEY ALWAYS HAVE.

those things left unsaid.

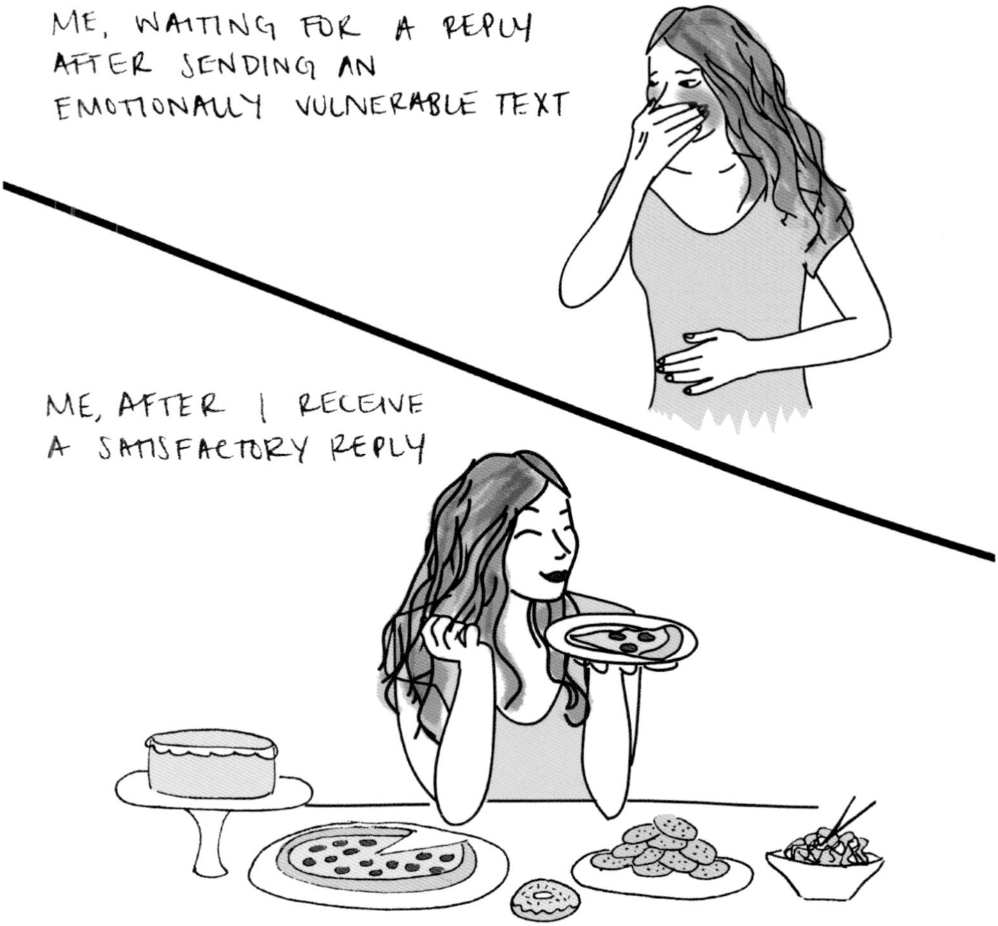
ME, WAITING FOR A REPLY AFTER SENDING AN EMOTIONALLY VULNERABLE TEXT
ME, AFTER I RECEIVE A SATISFACTORY REPLY

the relief spreads, and so does my appetite.

agony / ecstasy

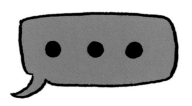

the best/worst invention.

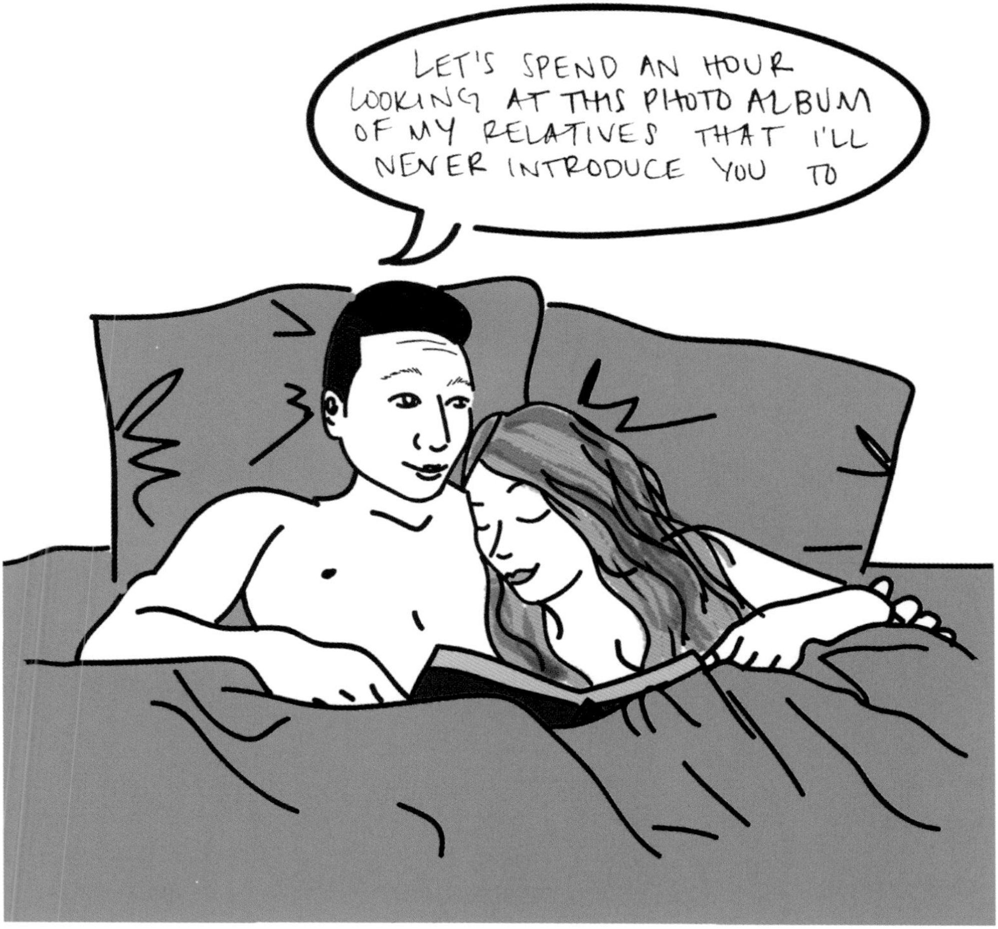
LET'S SPEND AN HOUR LOOKING AT THIS PHOTO ALBUM OF MY RELATIVES THAT I'LL NEVER INTRODUCE YOU TO

because that's not confusing at all.

my hero.

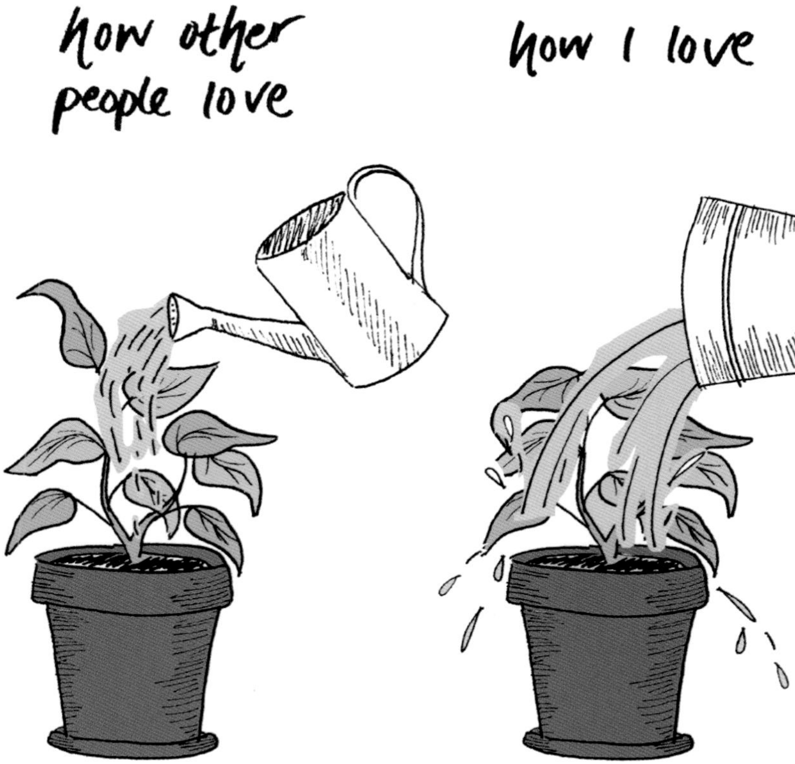
how other people love
how I love

why are all of my plants dead?

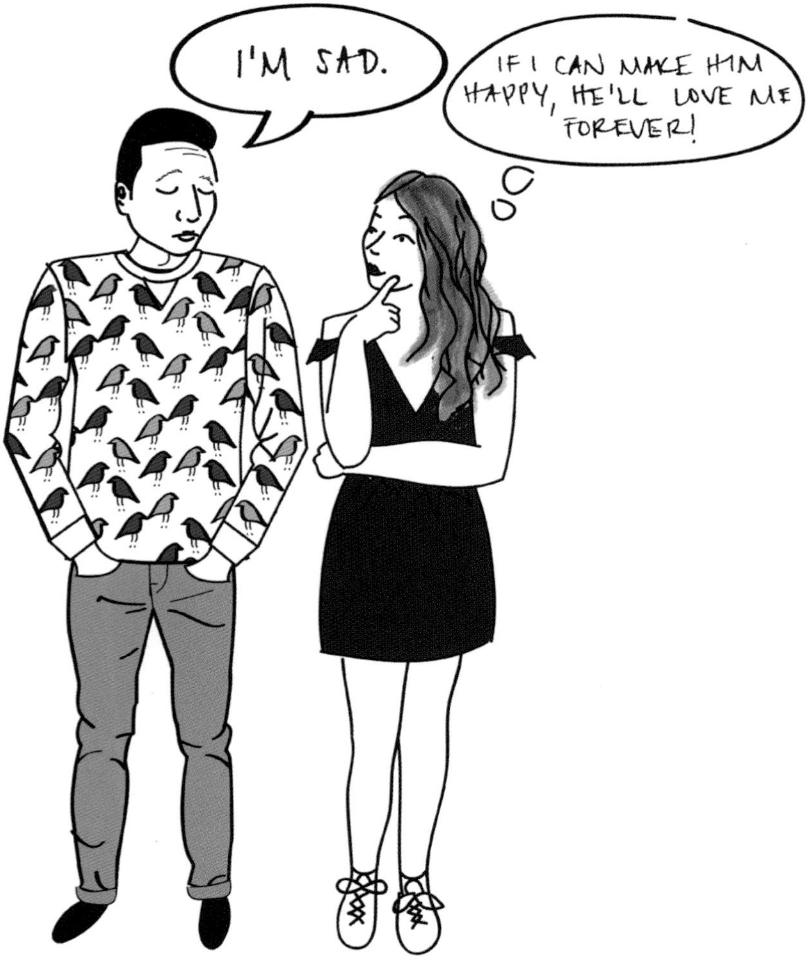
I'M SAD.
IF I CAN MAKE HIM HAPPY, HE'LL LOVE ME FOREVER!

what could go wrong?

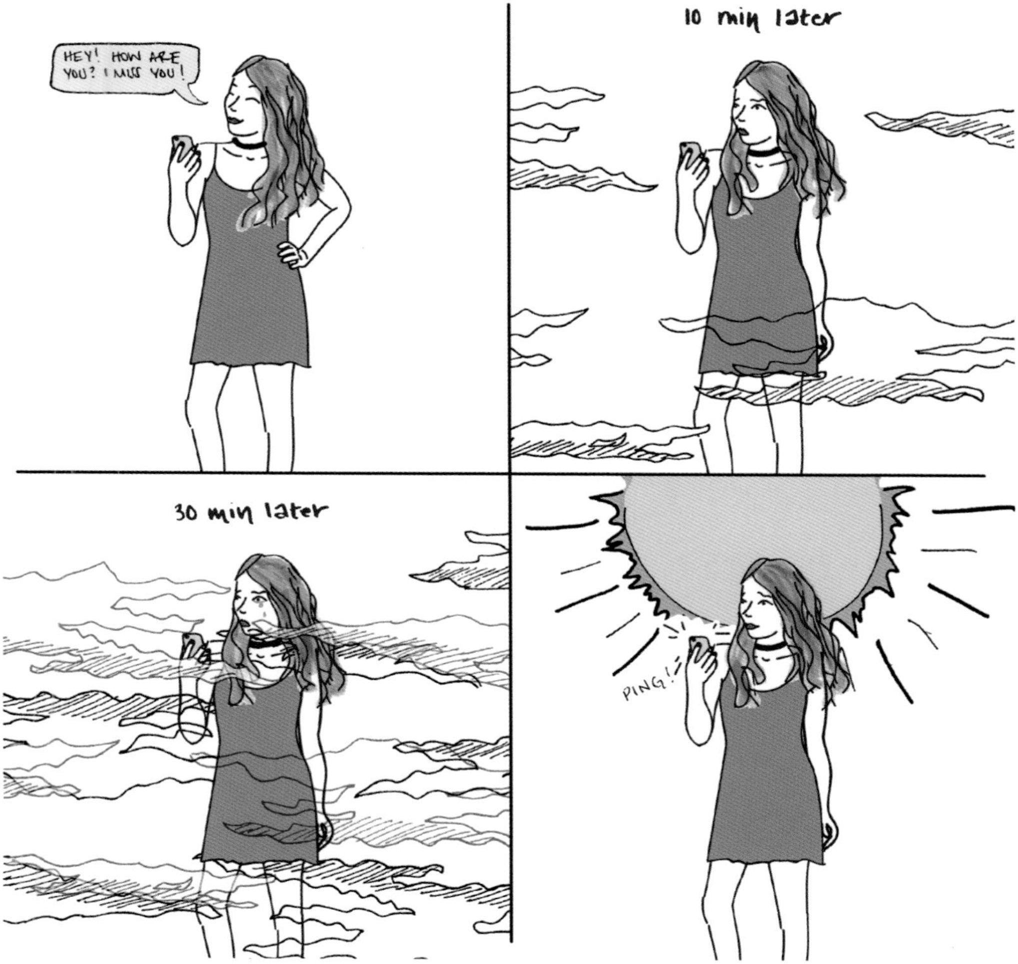
HEY! HOW ARE YOU? I MISS YOU!
10 min later
30 min later
PING!

we've got some inclement weather coming in.

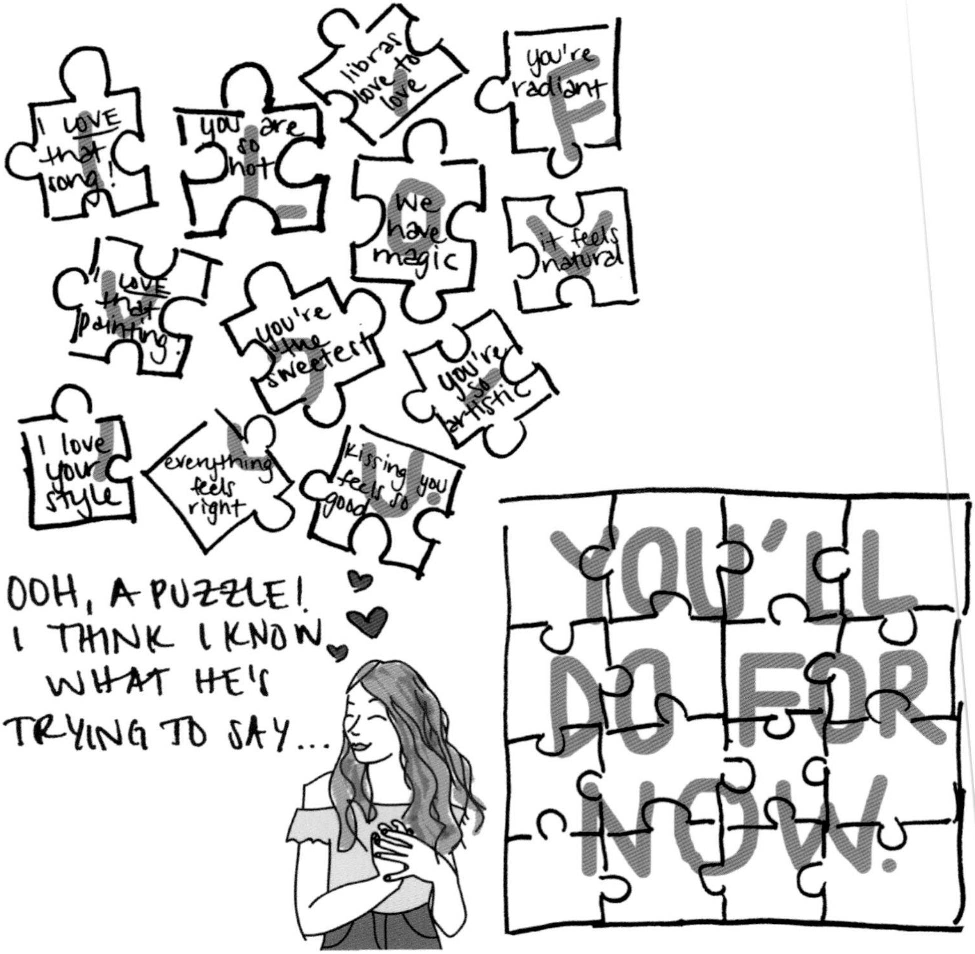
I LOVE that song!
you are so hot
libras love to love
you're radiant
we have magic
it feels natural
I LOVE that painting!
you're the sweetest
you're so artistic
I love your style
everything feels right
kissing you feels so good
OOH, A PUZZLE! I THINK I KNOW WHAT HE'S TRYING TO SAY...
YOU'LL DO FOR NOW.

wait a minute. . .

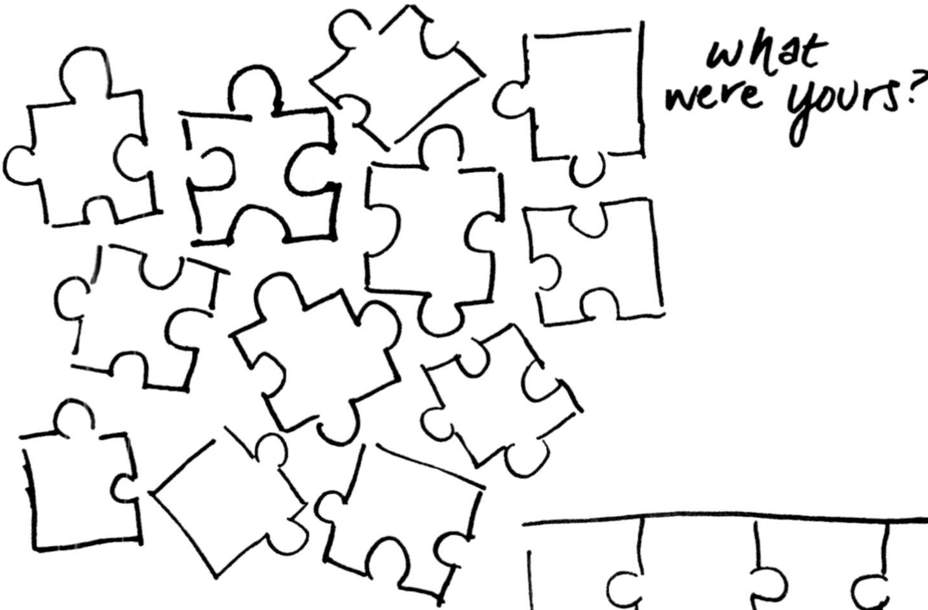
what were yours?

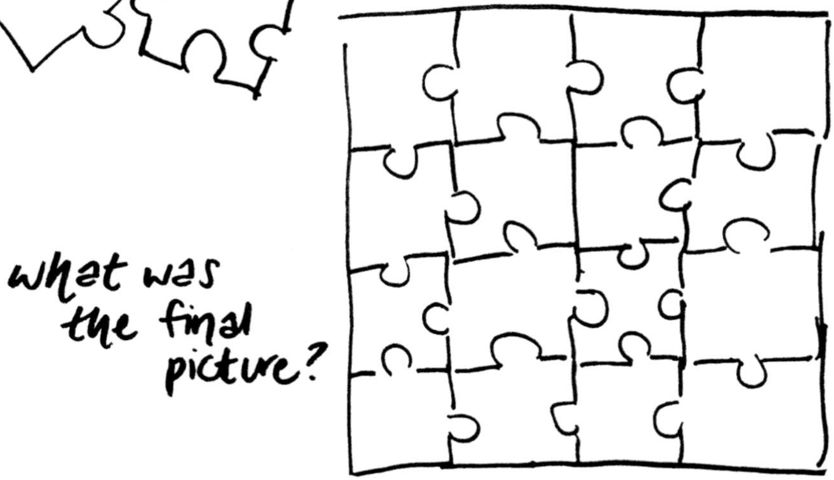
what was the final picture?

a relationship approach

OTHER PEOPLE

ME

DON'T RUSH IT

BURN, BABY, BURN

get that marshmallow in my mouth, stat.

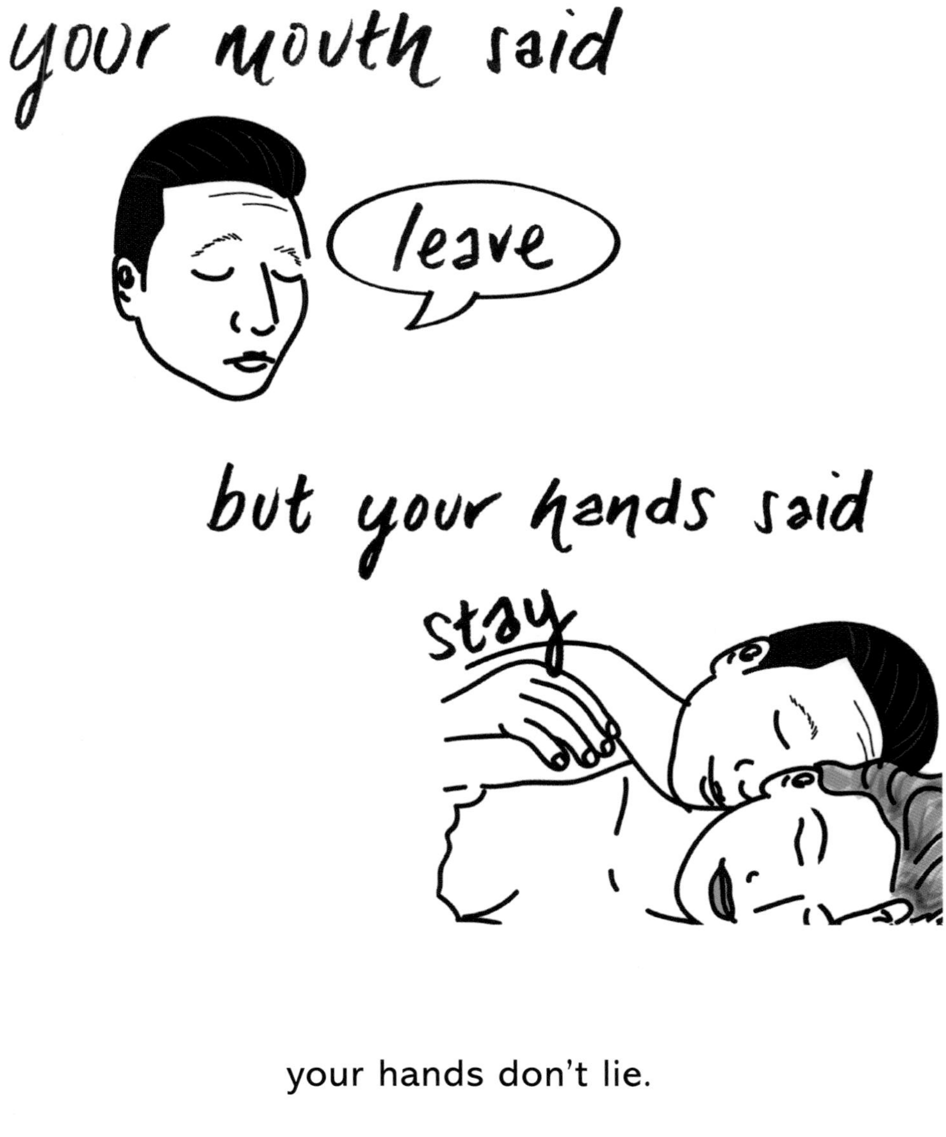
your mouth said
leave
but your hands said
stay

your hands don't lie.

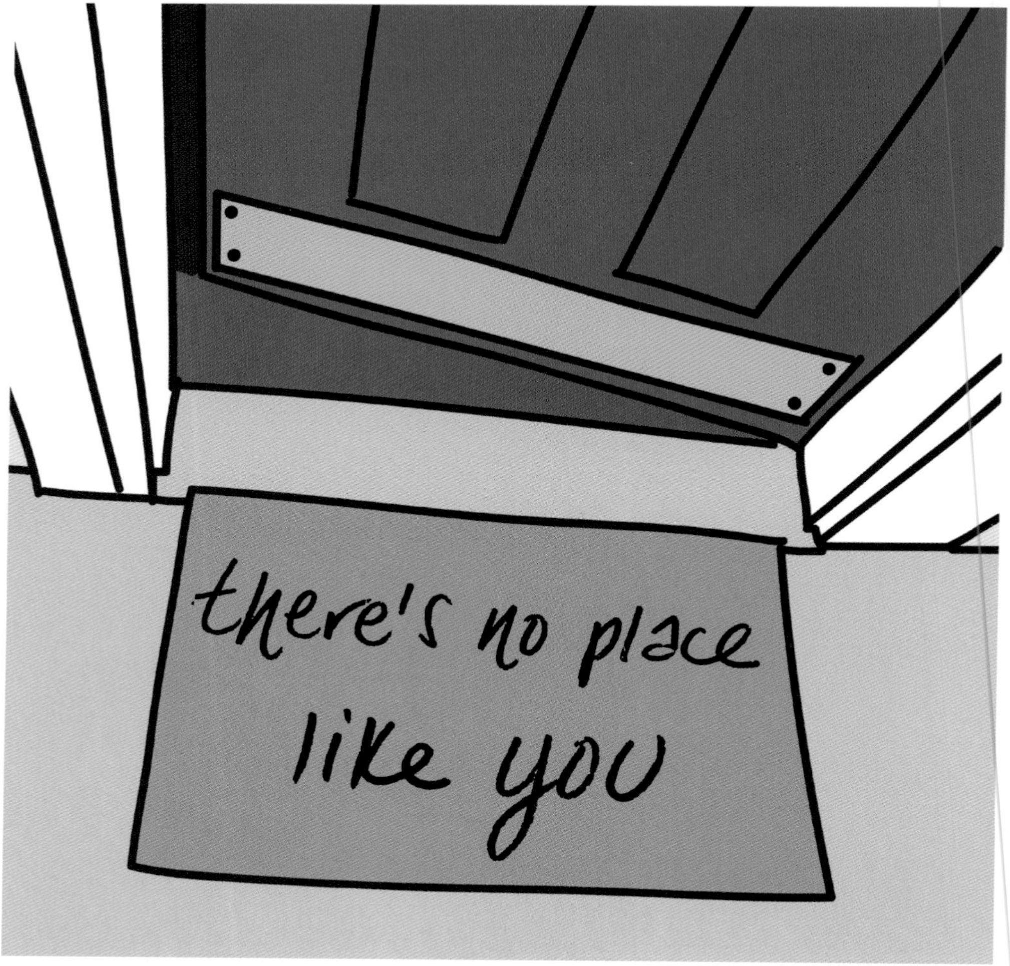
there's no place
like you

my happy place.

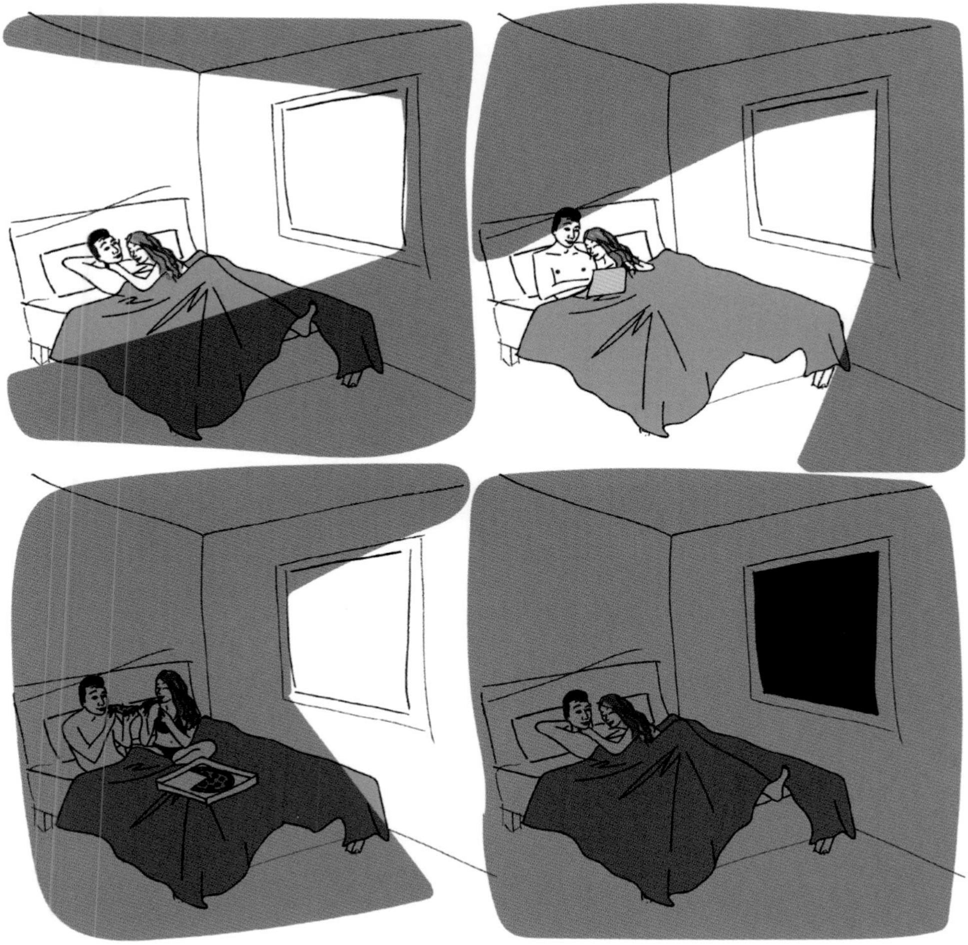

doing nothing with you was everything.

TINY CRACKS: WHEN DOUBTS BEGIN TO SURFACE

Have you ever had a tiny hunch that things weren't quite steady? And then you pushed that feeling down until you could no longer see it, at which point it was too late to get out unscathed? Yeah, I've done that, too. Those shattering moments make us realize, in hindsight, that we were the only ones who were all-in.

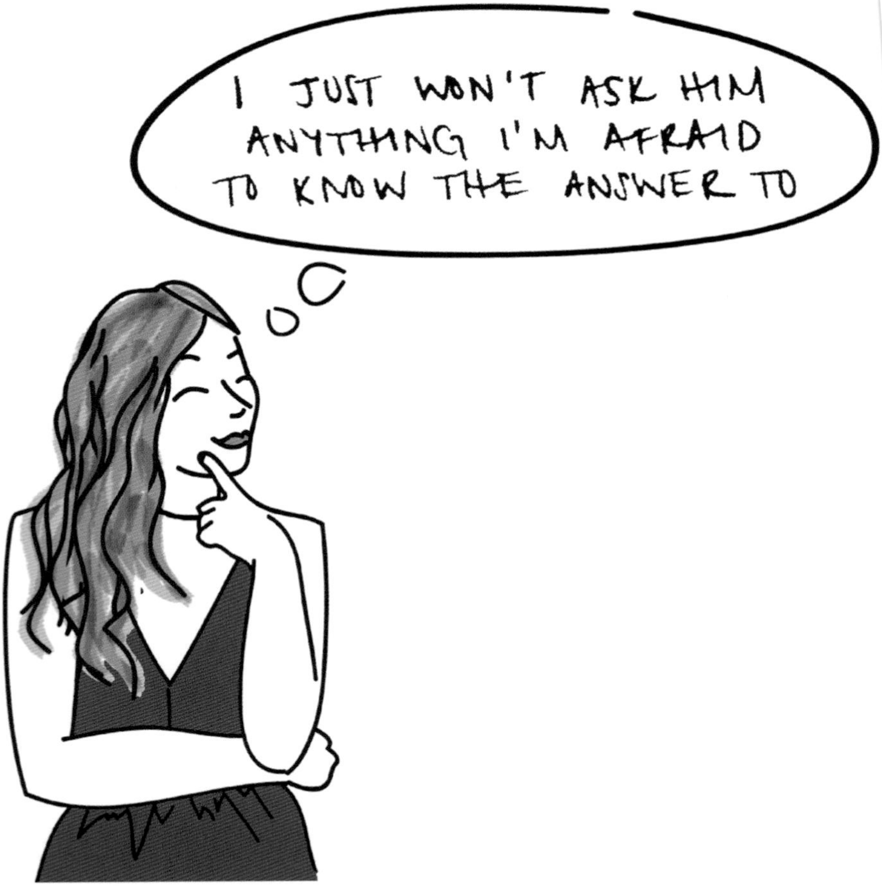
I JUST WON'T ASK HIM ANYTHING I'M AFRAID TO KNOW THE ANSWER TO

what you don't know can't hurt you, right?

lost in translation

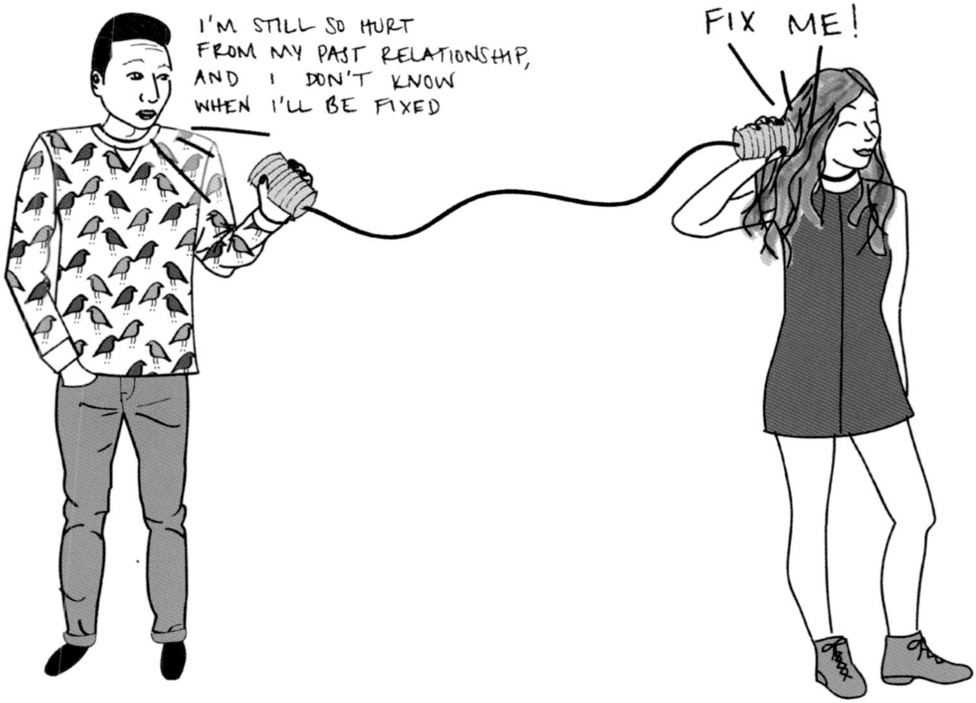

I'M STILL SO HURT FROM MY PAST RELATIONSHIP, AND I DON'T KNOW WHEN I'LL BE FIXED
FIX ME!

that's not what you said?

signs I clearly ignored

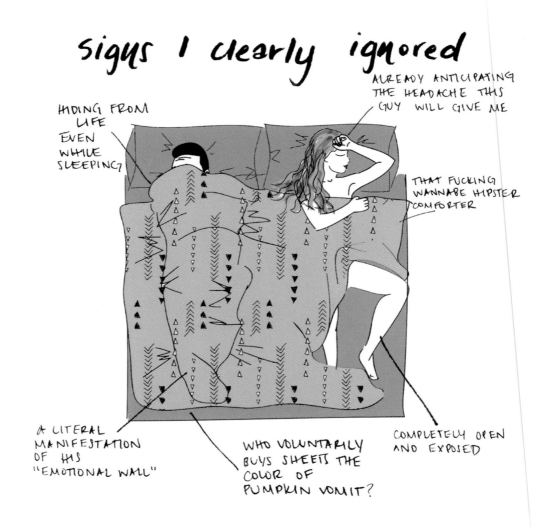

ALREADY ANTICIPATING THE HEADACHE THIS GUY WILL GIVE ME

HIDING FROM LIFE EVEN WHILE SLEEPING

THAT FUCKING WANNABE HIPSTER COMFORTER

A LITERAL MANIFESTATION OF HIS "EMOTIONAL WALL"

WHO VOLUNTARILY BUYS SHEETS THE COLOR OF PUMPKIN VOMIT?

COMPLETELY OPEN AND EXPOSED

even in sleep, you were a nightmare.

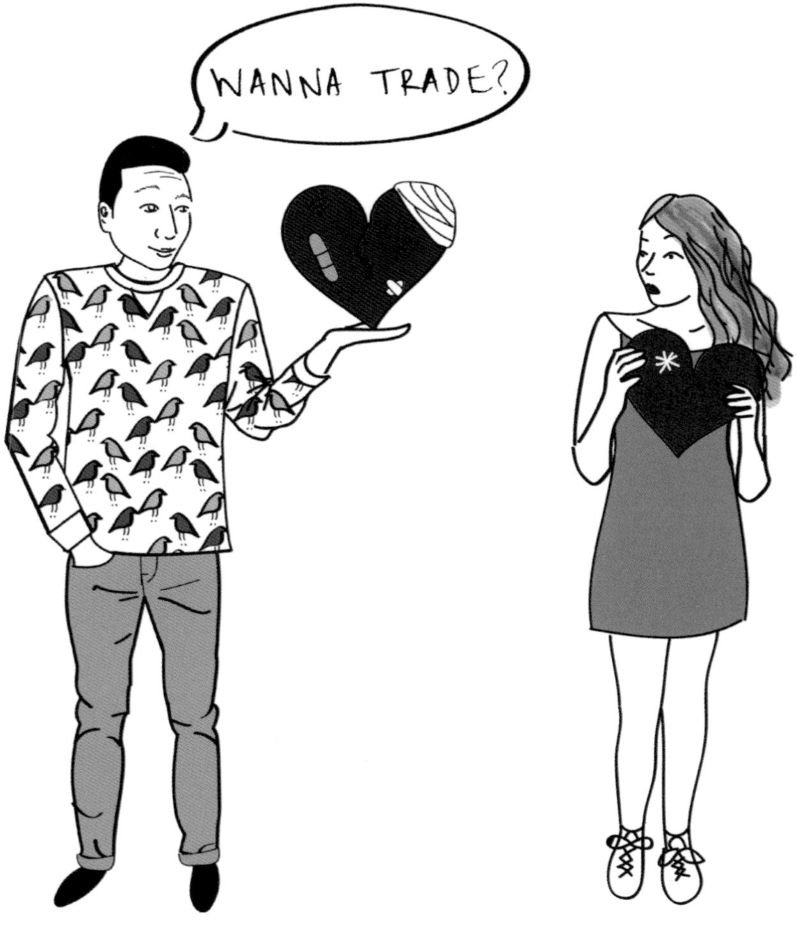
WANNA TRADE?

no no no no no.

things I pay attention to	things I overlook
MYERS – BRIGGS TYPE	GEOGRAPHIC LOCATION
ASTROLOGICAL COMPATIBILITY	DATING HISTORY
HOW OFTEN + ENTHUSIASTICALLY THEY COMPLIMENT ME	EMOTIONAL AVAILABILITY
WHETHER THEY APPRECIATE THE LYRICS OF MY FAVORITE SONGS	
AMBITION	
WILLINGNESS TO SHARE FOOD	

priorities.

what did you pay attention to?   what did you overlook?

YOU ARE GORGEOUS
WITHOUT MAKEUP

I HAVE A WALL UP,
AND IT CAN'T
COME DOWN FOR
A WHILE

STAY AT LONG
AS YOU LIKE

I NEED TIME
AND SPACE

EVERYTHING ABOUT
THIS JUST FEELS RIGHT

I DON'T KNOW
WHAT I WANT

BEING WITH YOU IS
SO COMFORTABLE

I DON'T LIKE MYSELF
MOST DAYS

I'M SO IMPRESSED BY YOU

getting a bit carsick over here.

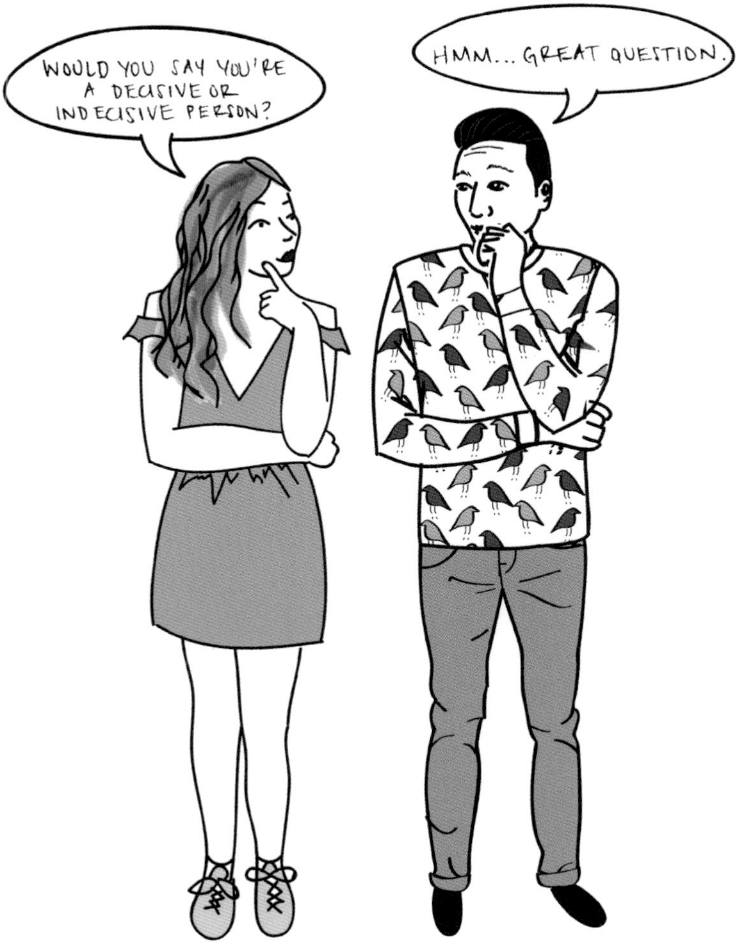
WOULD YOU SAY YOU'RE A DECISIVE OR INDECISIVE PERSON?
HMM... GREAT QUESTION.

great answer.

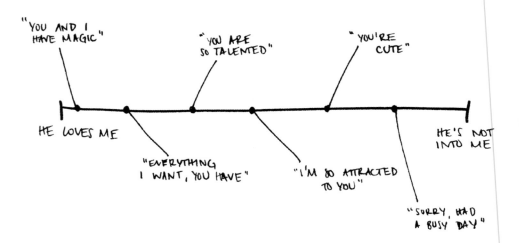

"YOU AND I
HAVE MAGIC"

" YOU ARE
SO TALENTED"

" YOU'RE
CUTE"

HE LOVES ME

"EVERYTHING
I WANT, YOU HAVE"

"I'M SO ATTRACTED
TO YOU"

HE'S NOT
INTO ME

"SORRY, HAD
A BUSY DAY"

a daily spectrum.

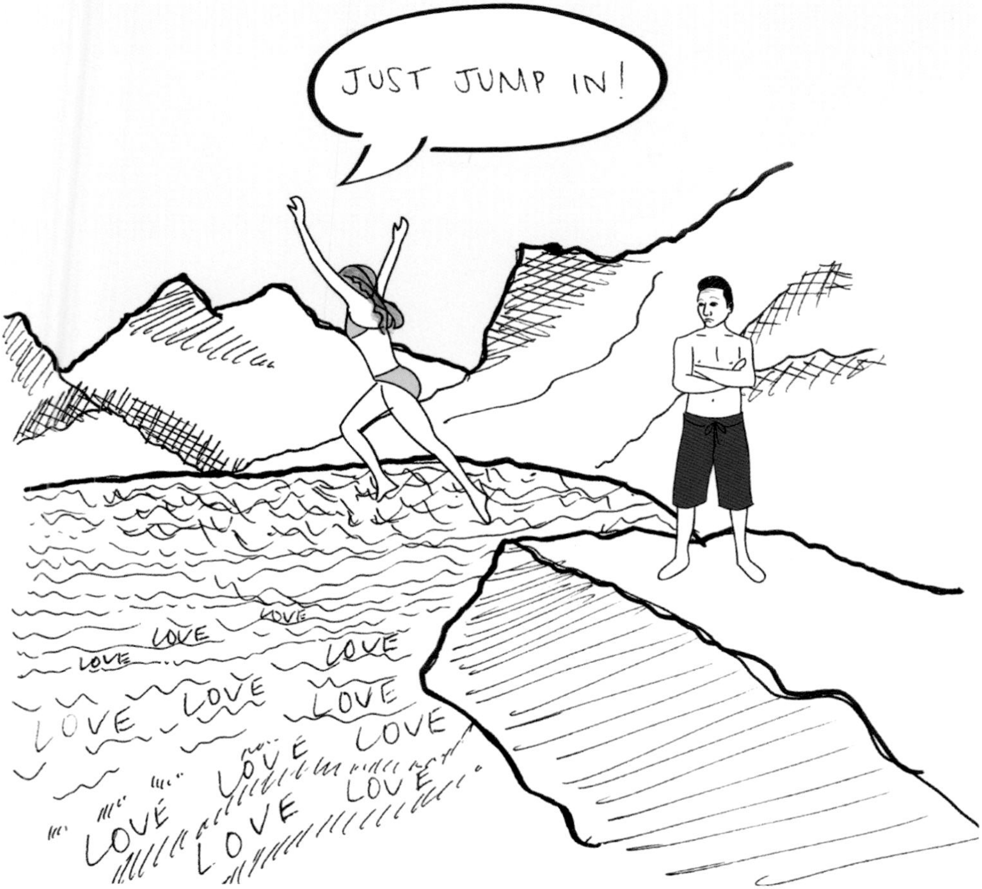
JUST JUMP IN!
LOVE LOVE LOVE LOVE LOVE LOVE LOVE LOVE LOVE LOVE LOVE LOVE LOVE

I'm that asshole who insists on swimming
when no one else wants to.

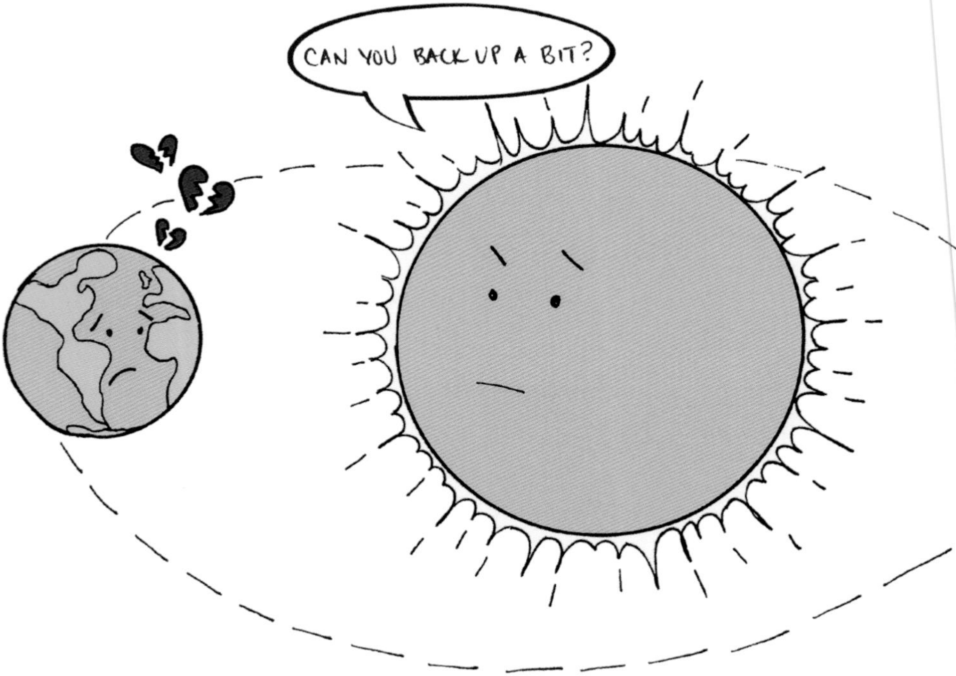
CAN YOU BACK UP A BIT?

I'm kind of stuck here.

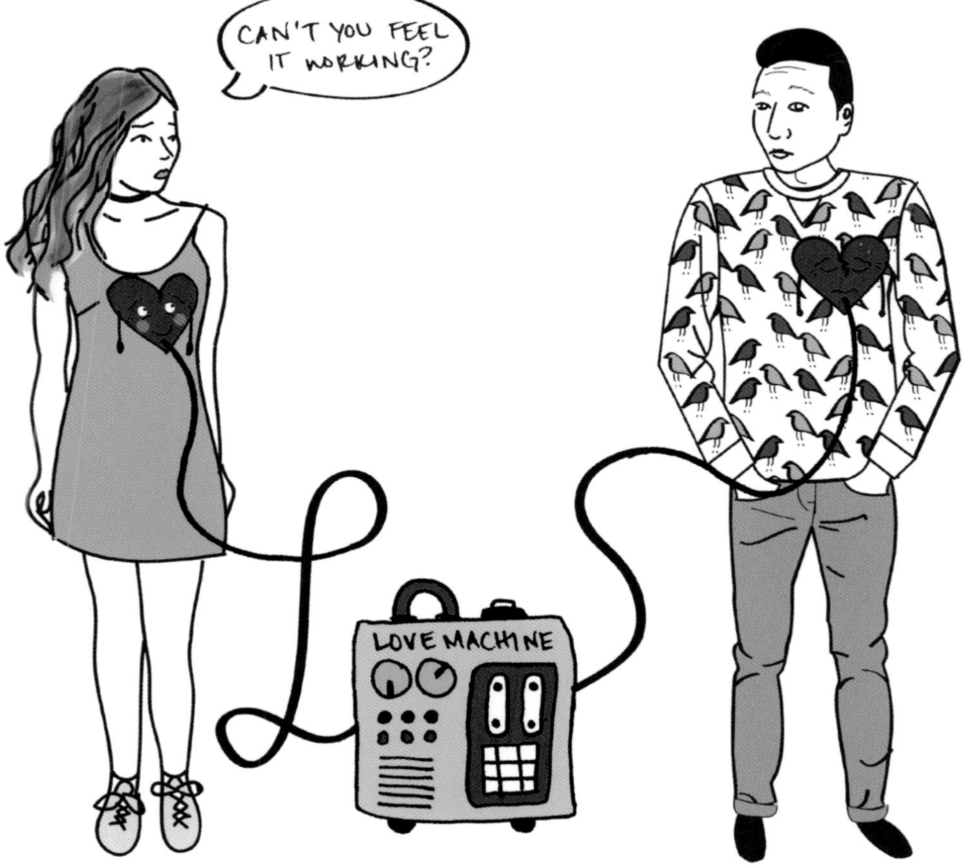
CAN'T YOU FEEL IT WORKING?
LOVE MACHINE

is it plugged in?

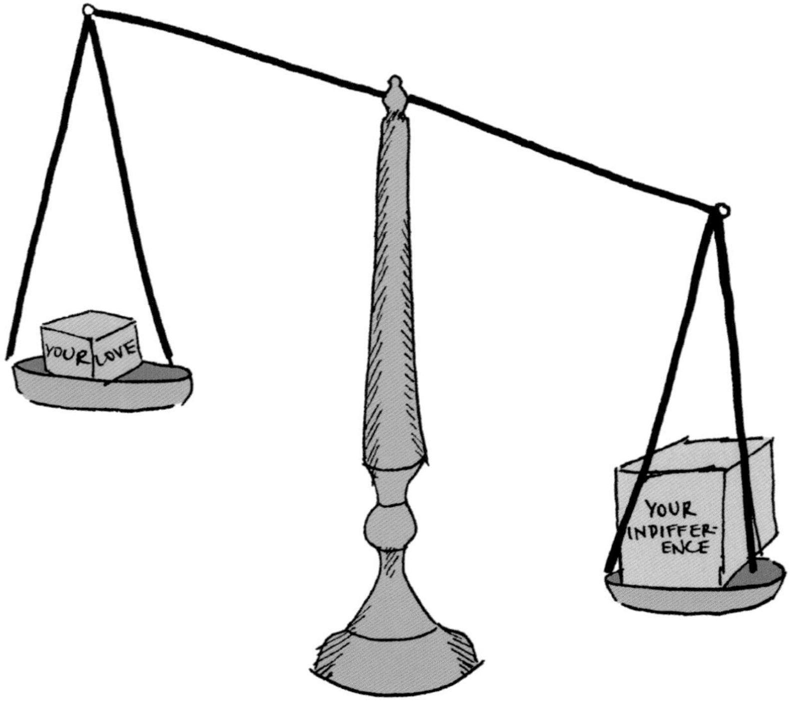
YOUR LOVE
YOUR INDIFFERENCE

heavy.

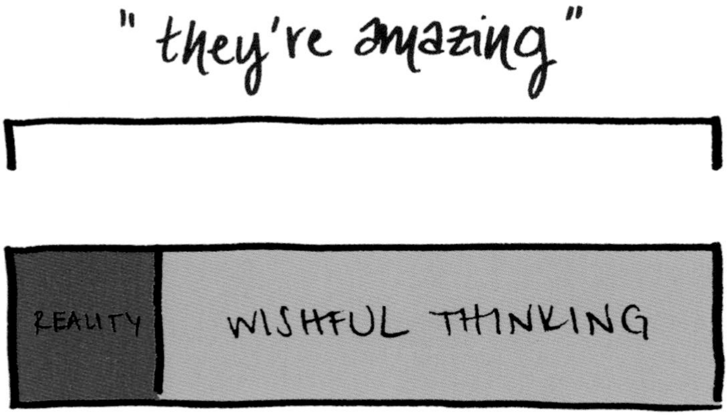
" they're amazing "
REALITY
WISHFUL THINKING

just keep wishin'.

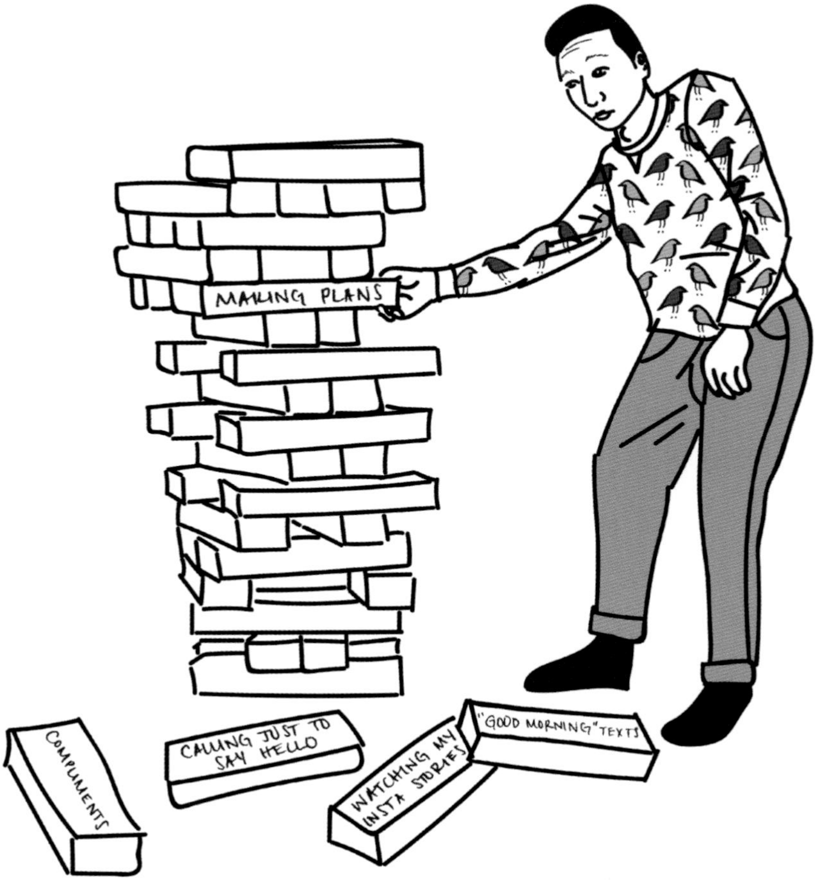
MAKING PLANS
COMPLIMENTS
CALLING JUST TO SAY HELLO
WATCHING MY INSTA STORIES
"GOOD MORNING" TEXTS

why did you build it, then?

what were the first
pieces to fall?

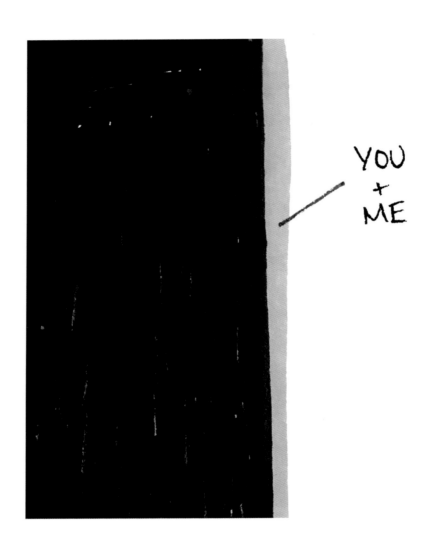

always cozy in that gray area.

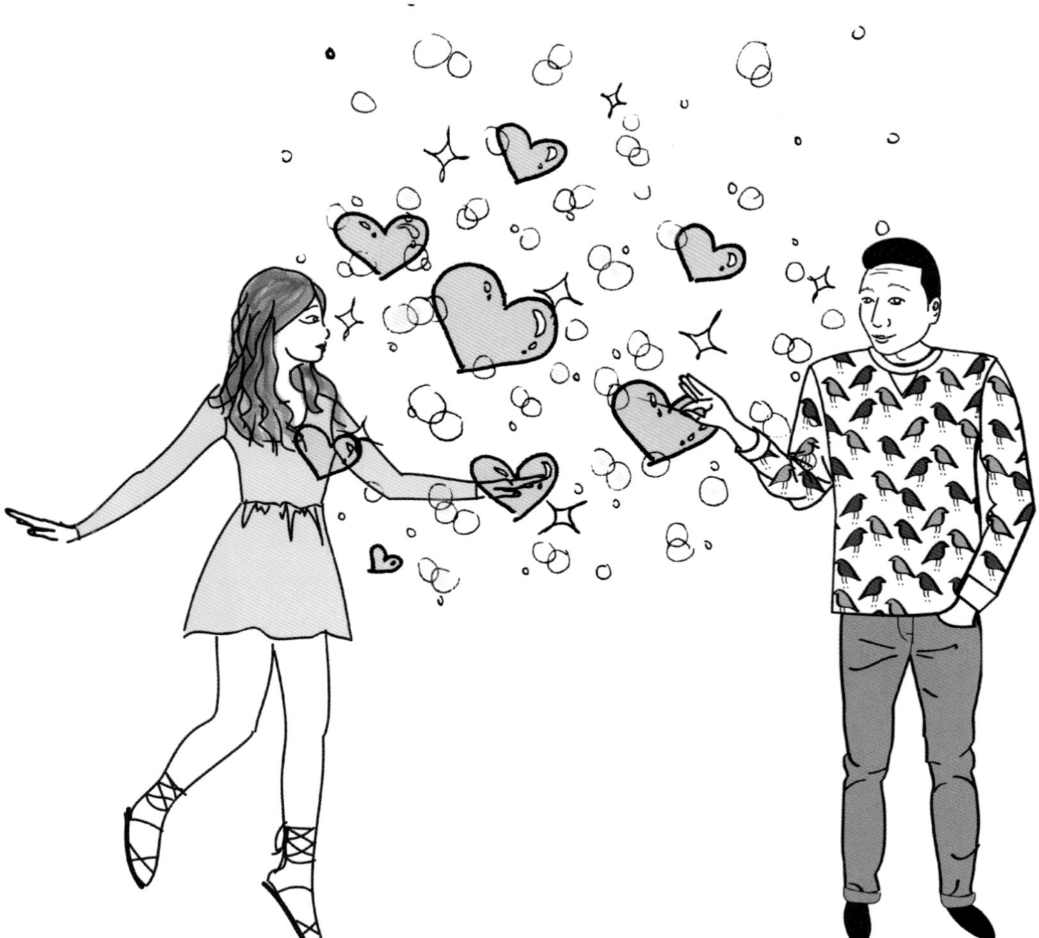

pop pop pop.

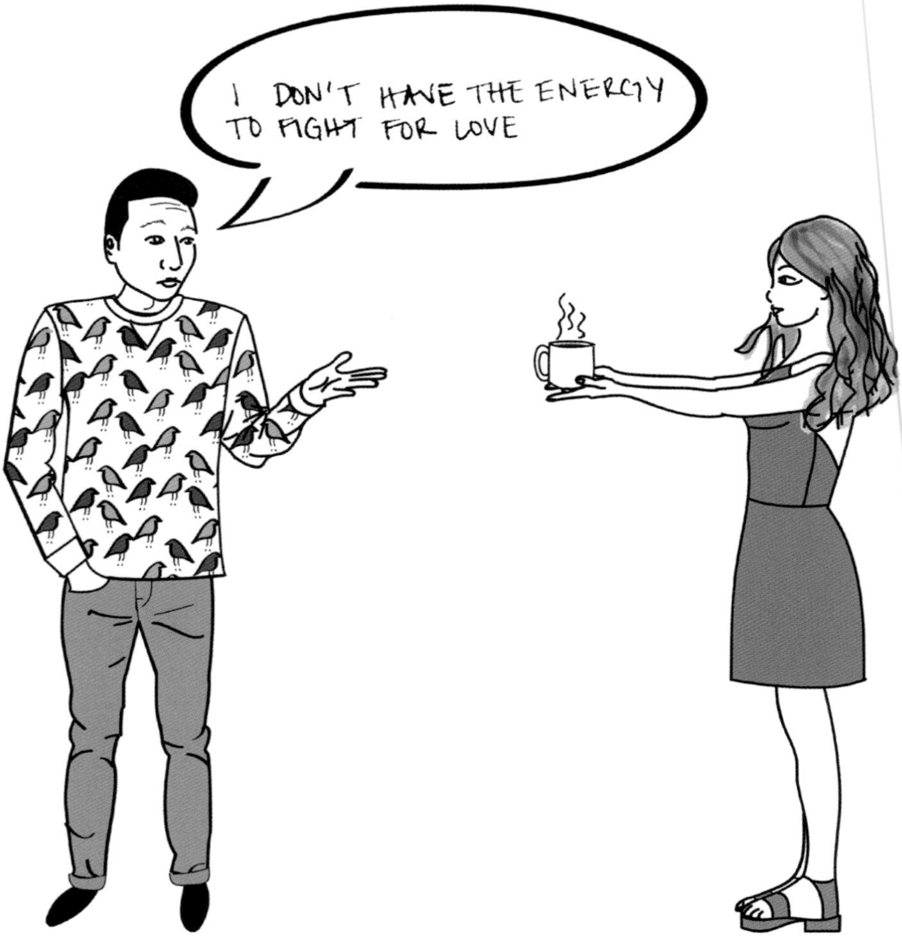
I DON'T HAVE THE ENERGY TO FIGHT FOR LOVE

cream and sugar?

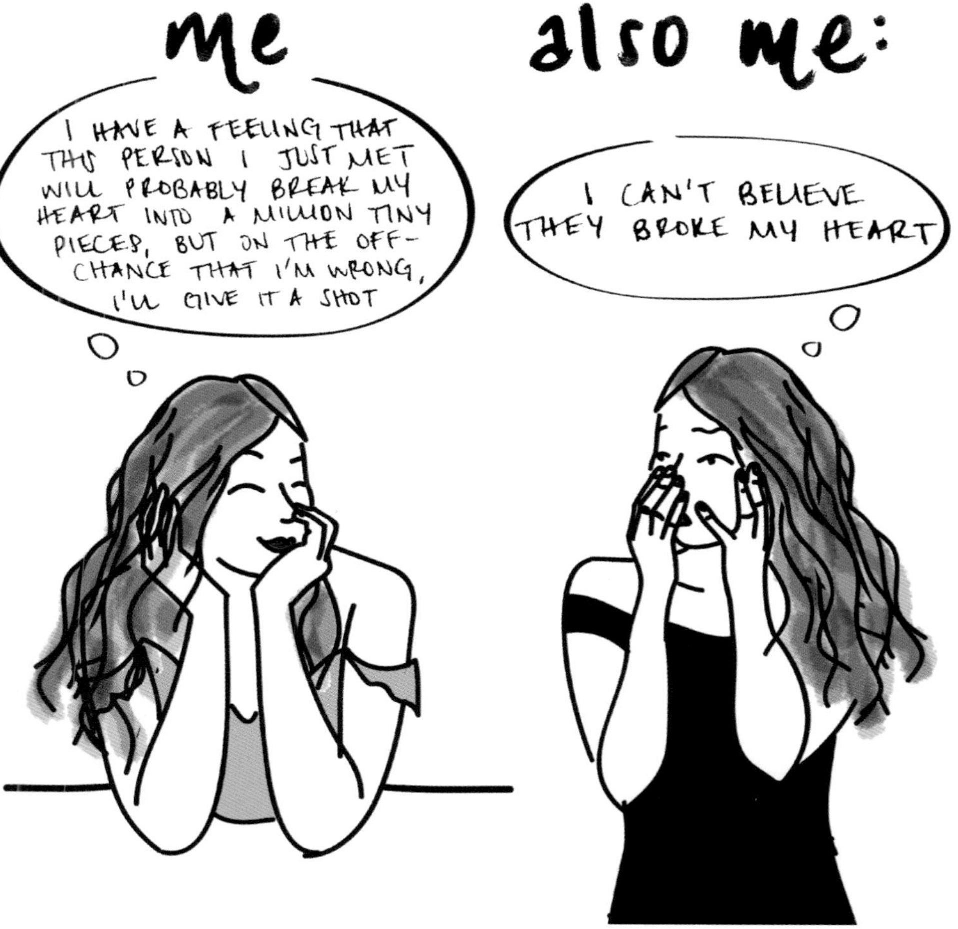
me
also me:
I HAVE A FEELING THAT THIS PERSON I JUST MET WILL PROBABLY BREAK MY HEART INTO A MILLION TINY PIECES, BUT ON THE OFF-CHANCE THAT I'M WRONG, I'LL GIVE IT A SHOT
I CAN'T BELIEVE THEY BROKE MY HEART

hopelessly optimistic.

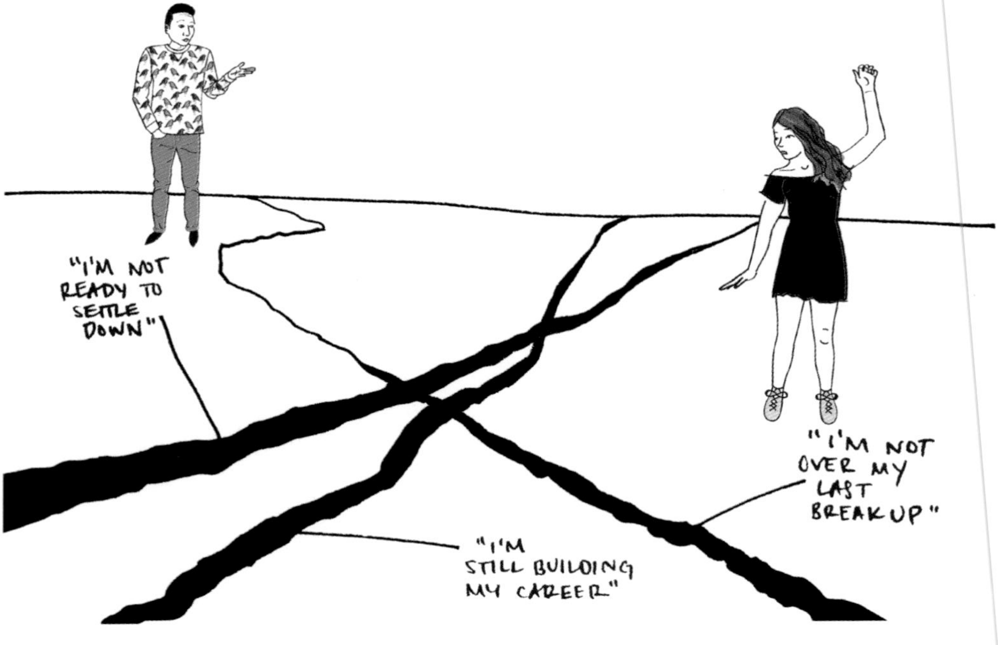
"I'M NOT READY TO SETTLE DOWN"
"I'M NOT OVER MY LAST BREAKUP"
"I'M STILL BUILDING MY CAREER"

check the Richter.

what caused
your cracks?

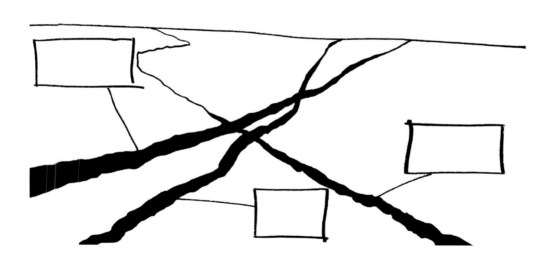

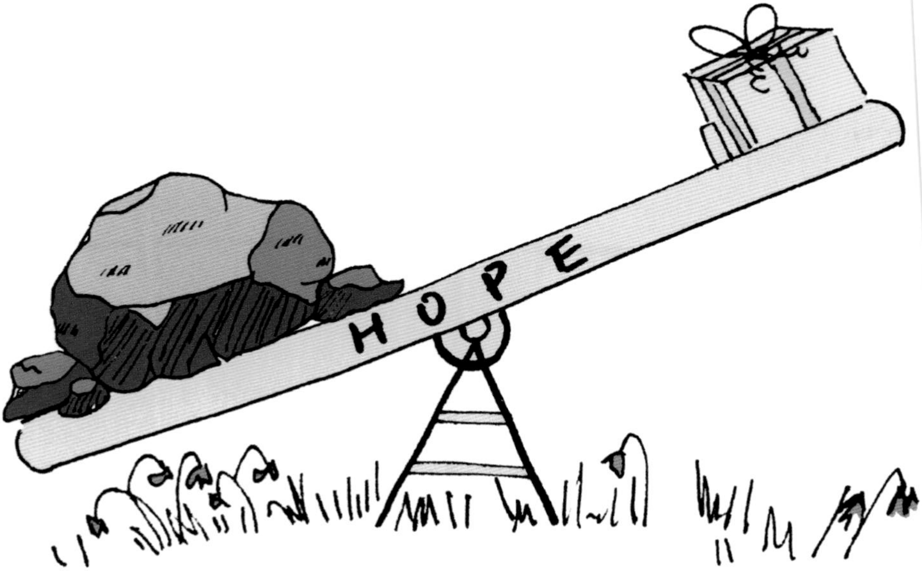
HOPE

not a gift anymore.

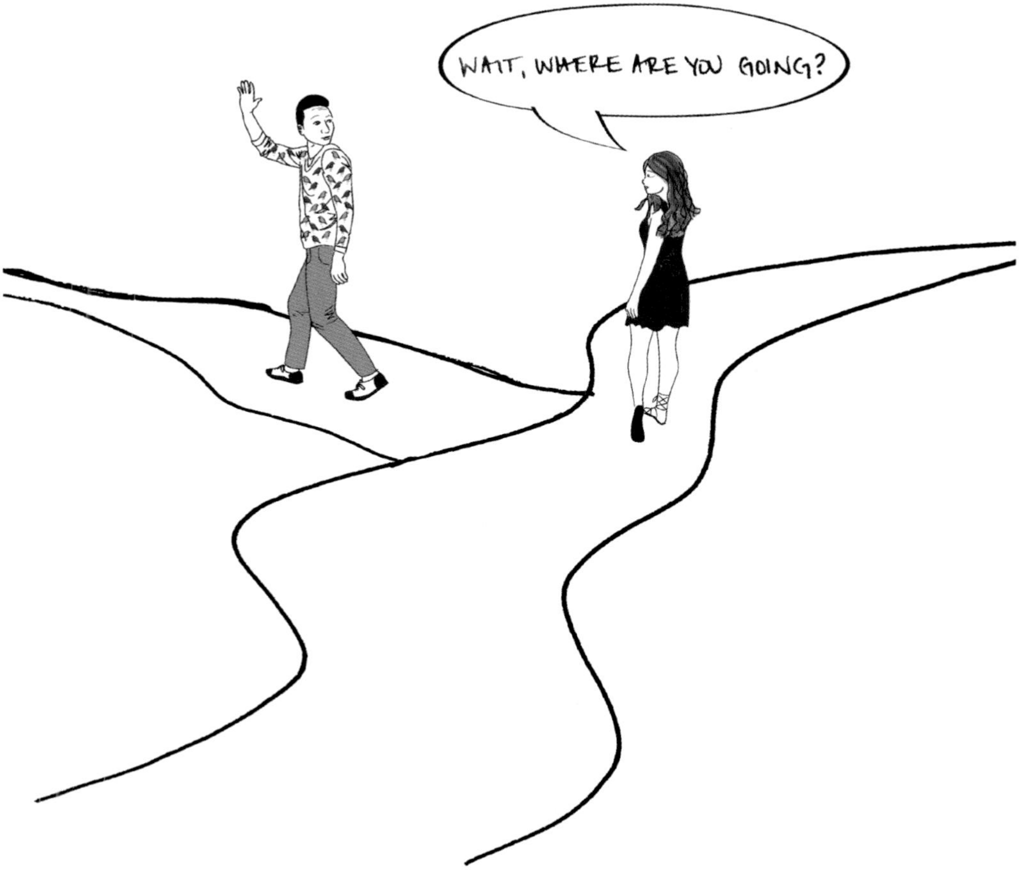
WAIT, WHERE ARE YOU GOING?

but my GPS says we should keep going right . . .

IF YOU CAN'T, WE CAN'T: THE COLLAPSE COMES SWIFTLY AND CRUELLY

"I'm not ready for a relationship right now."

"I need to focus on myself."

"I care about you, but I don't love you."

Remember those red flags I ignored? No matter how it's said, hearing we aren't loved or wanted is never easy. Our world comes crashing down, and we're left alone, picking up the pieces of ourselves. The best we can do is try to find humor in the breakdown.

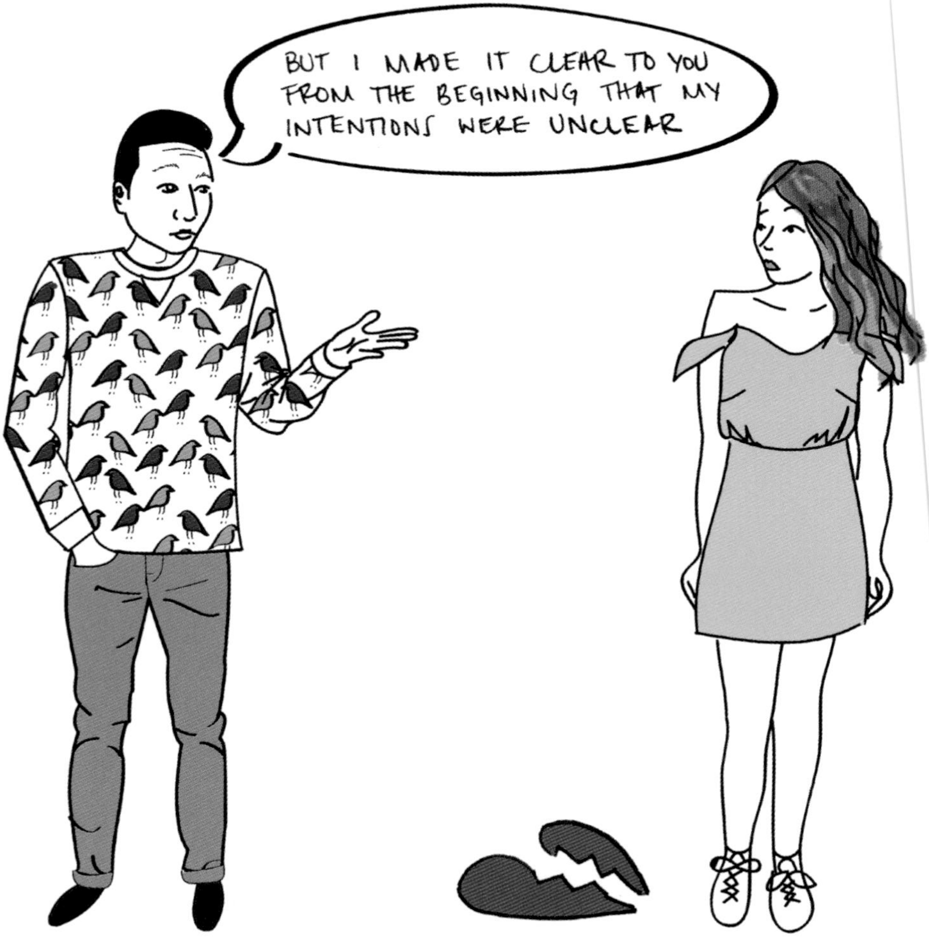
BUT I MADE IT CLEAR TO YOU FROM THE BEGINNING THAT MY INTENTIONS WERE UNCLEAR

clearly.

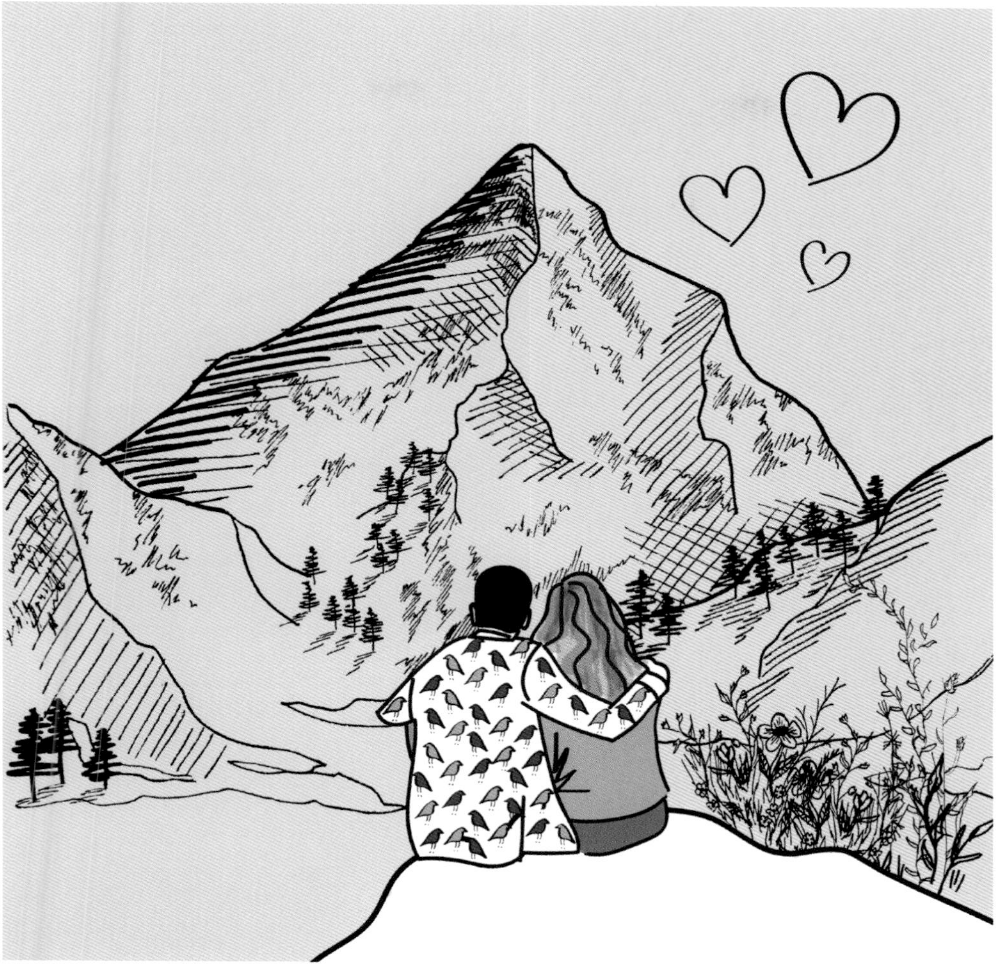

two different worlds.

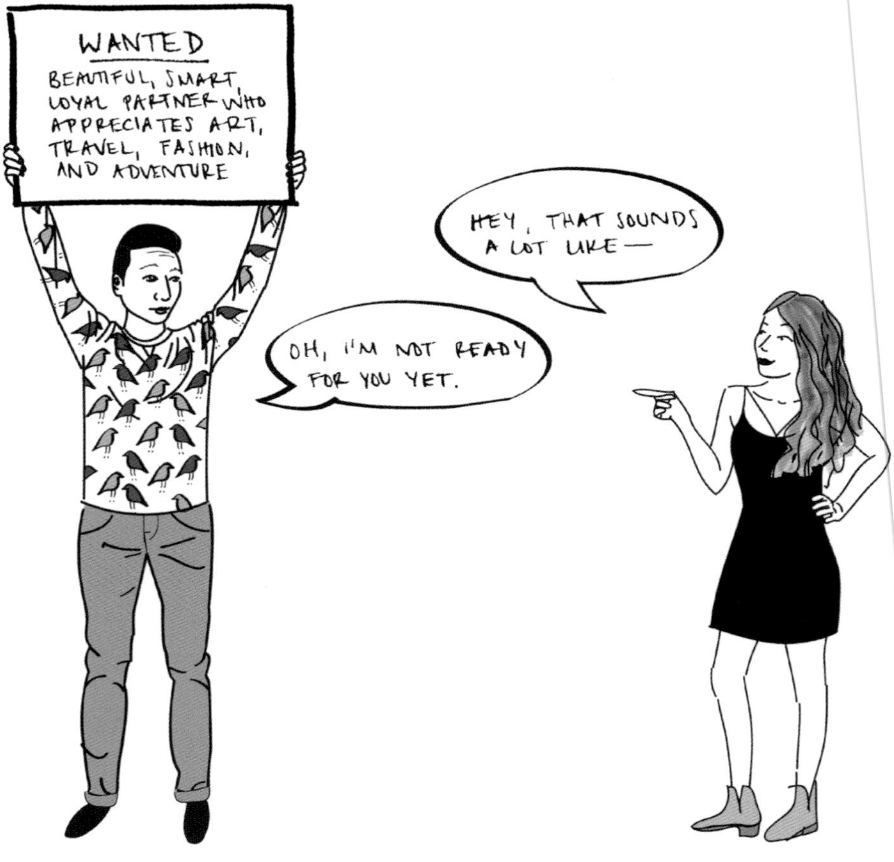
WANTED
BEAUTIFUL, SMART, LOYAL PARTNER WHO APPRECIATES ART, TRAVEL, FASHION, AND ADVENTURE
HEY, THAT SOUNDS A LOT LIKE—
OH, I'M NOT READY FOR YOU YET.

. . . me.

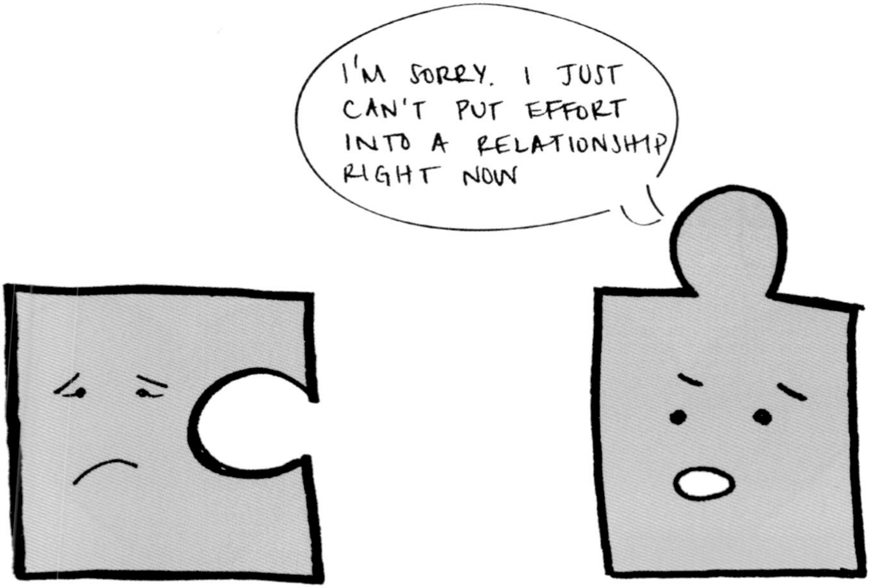
I'M SORRY. I JUST CAN'T PUT EFFORT INTO A RELATIONSHIP RIGHT NOW

the world's most difficult puzzle.

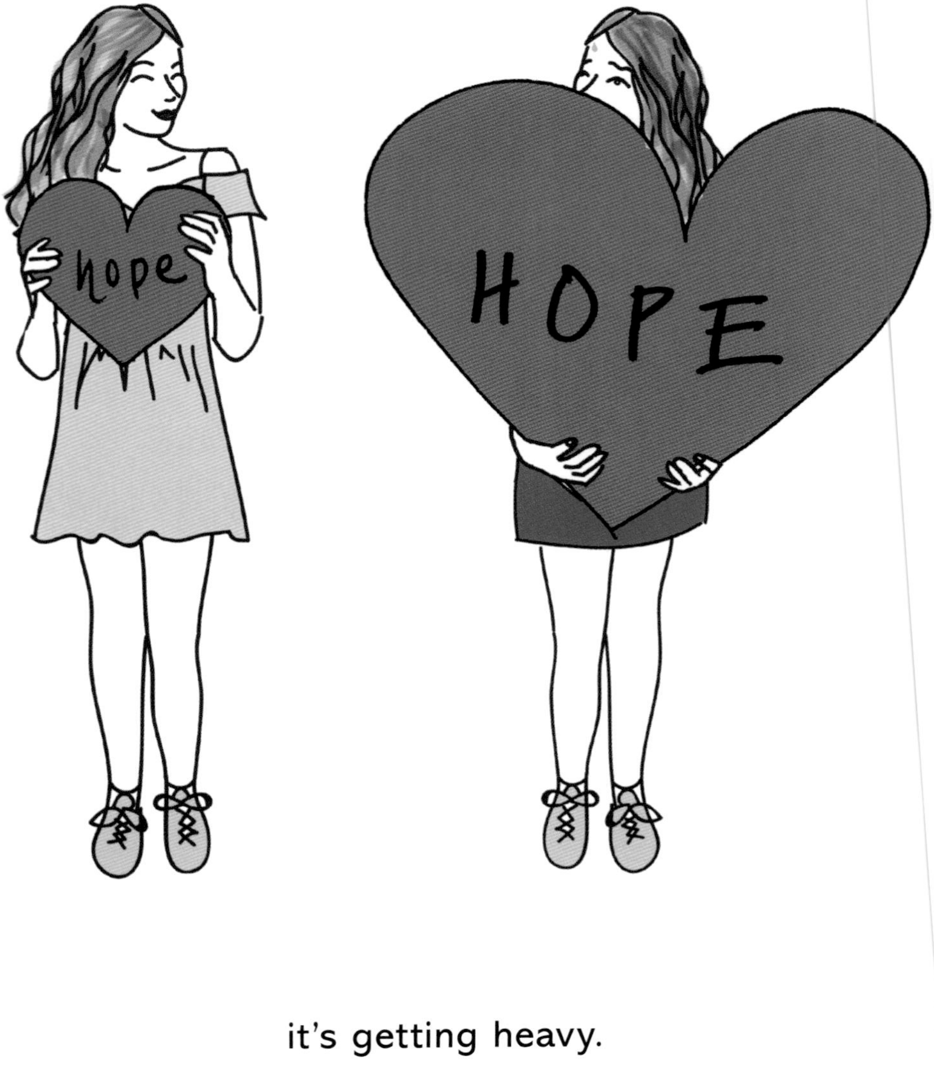
hope
HOPE

it's getting heavy.

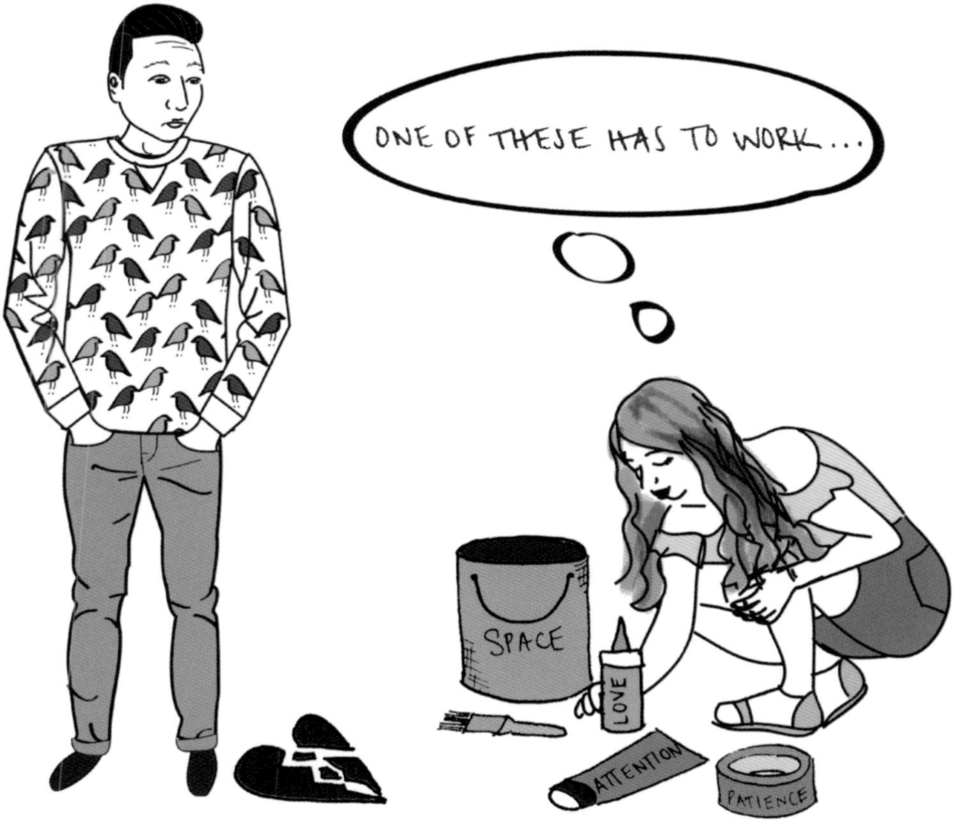
ONE OF THESE HAS TO WORK...
SPACE
LOVE
ATTENTION
PATIENCE

I've always been pretty handy.

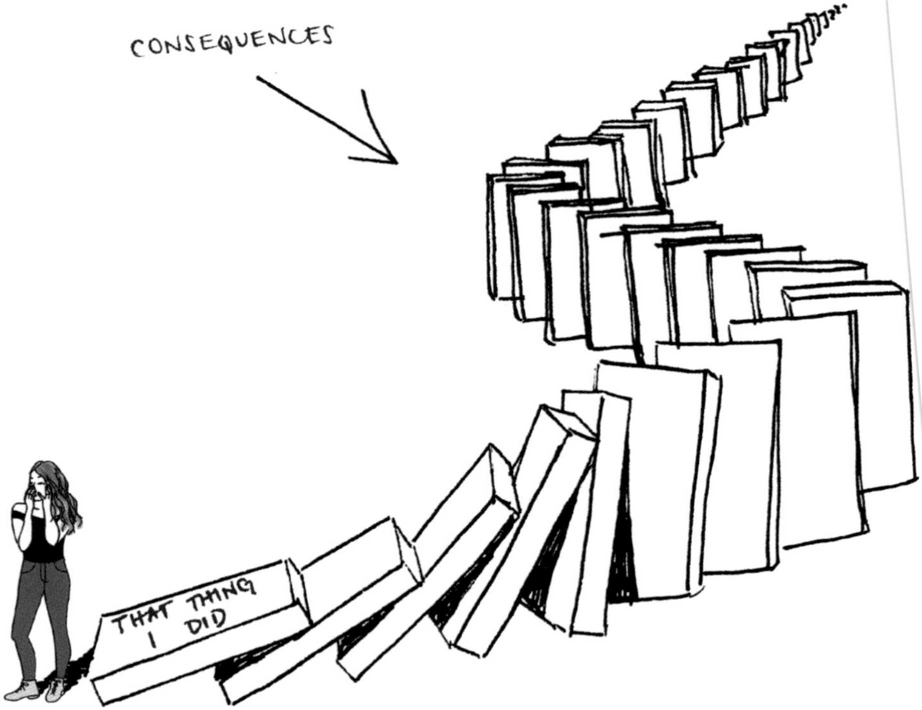
CONSEQUENCES
THAT THING I DID

timber.

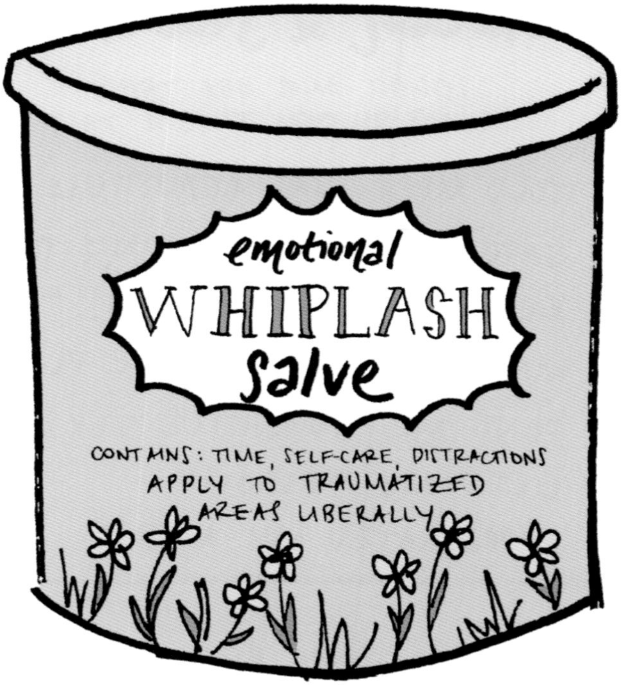
emotional
WHIPLASH
salve
CONTAINS: TIME, SELF-CARE, DISTRACTIONS
APPLY TO TRAUMATIZED
AREAS LIBERALLY

for my aches and pains.

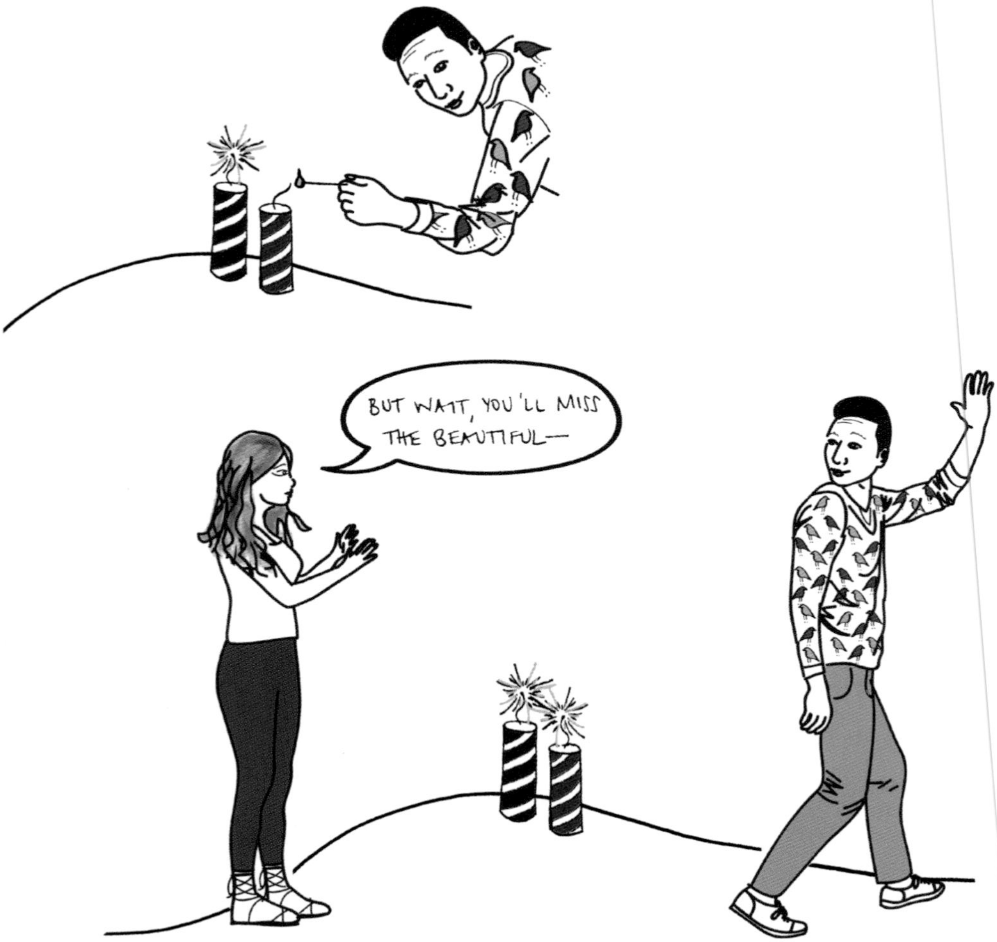
BUT WAIT, YOU'LL MISS THE BEAUTIFUL—

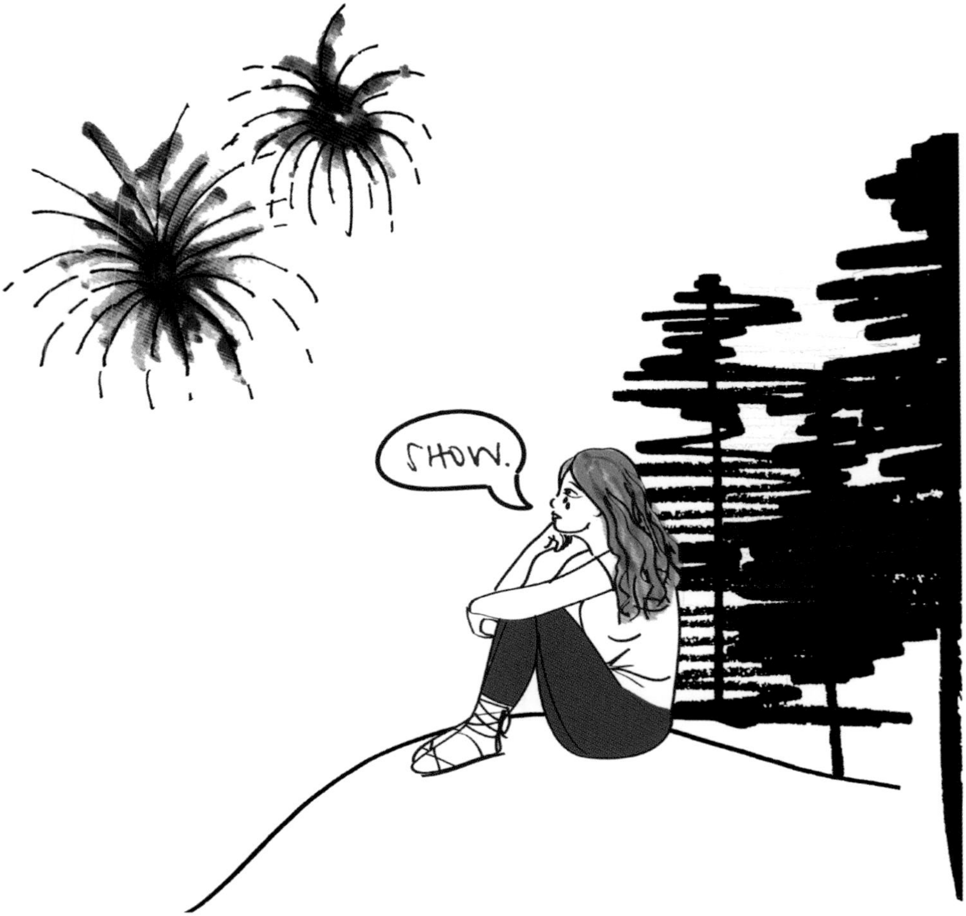
SHOW.

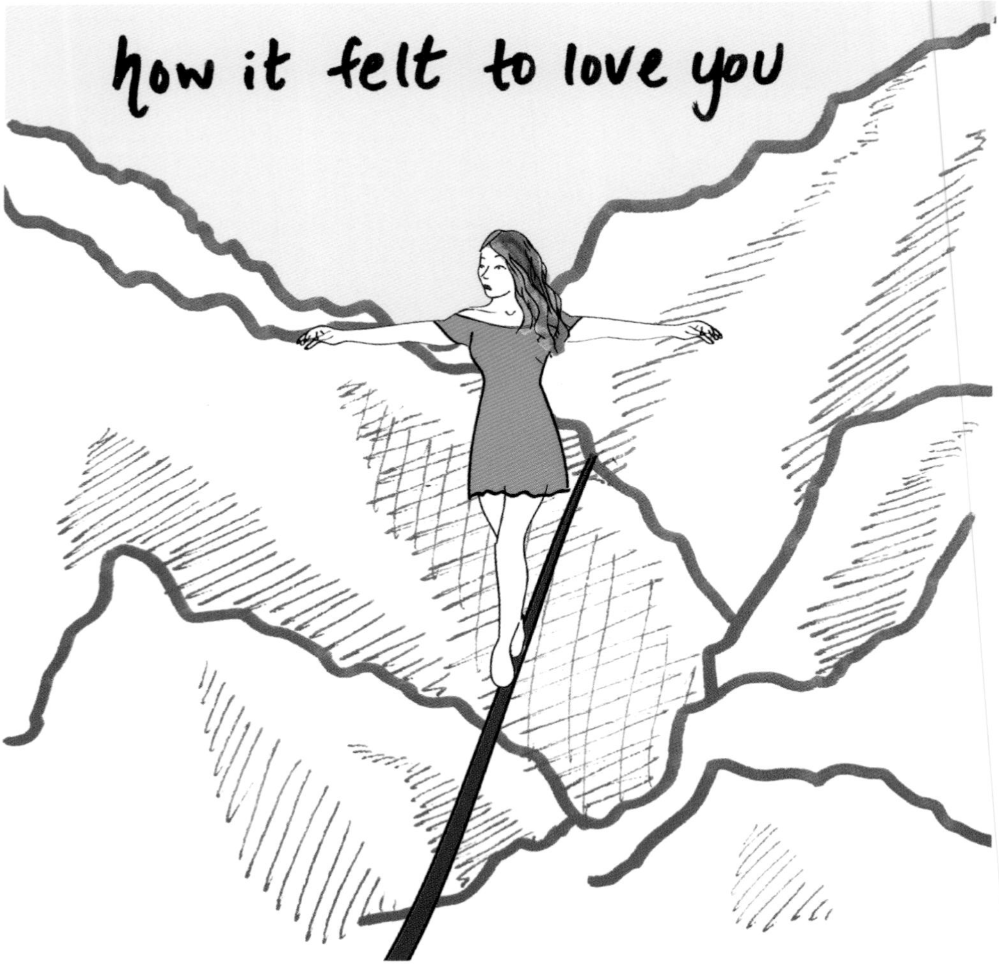
how it felt to love you

good thing I'm not afraid of heights.

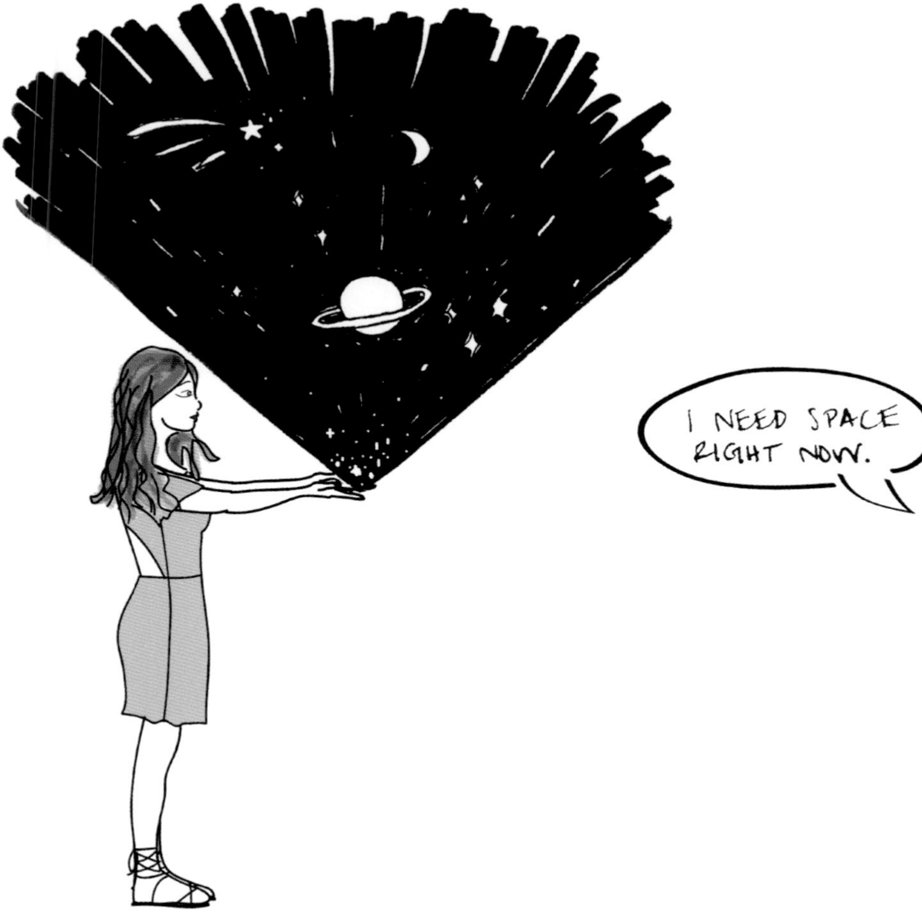
I NEED SPACE RIGHT NOW.

I'd give you the universe if you'd let me in.

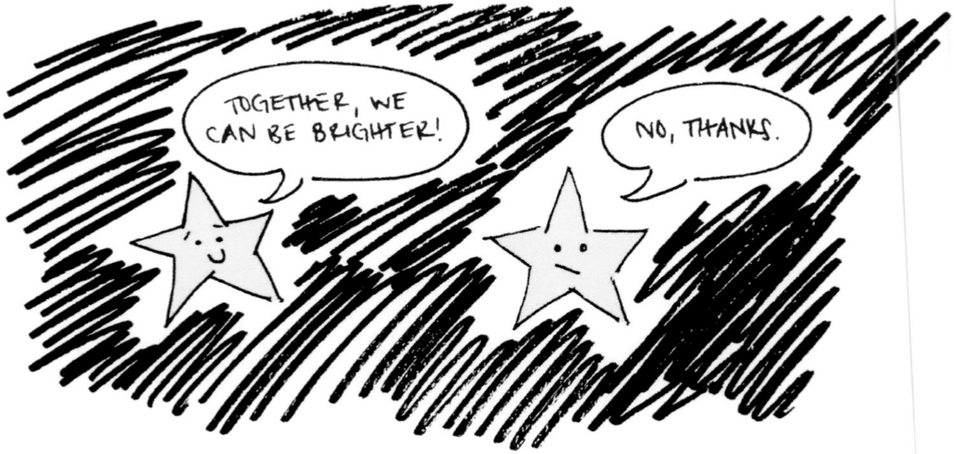
TOGETHER, WE CAN BE BRIGHTER!
NO, THANKS.

oh, ok.

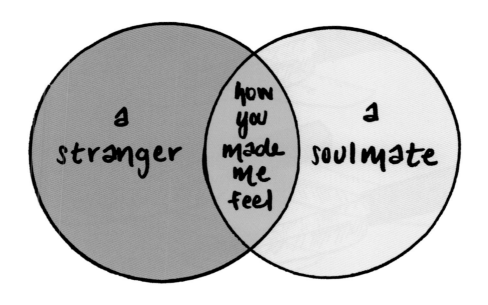

a stranger

how you made me feel

a soulmate

two sides of the same coin.

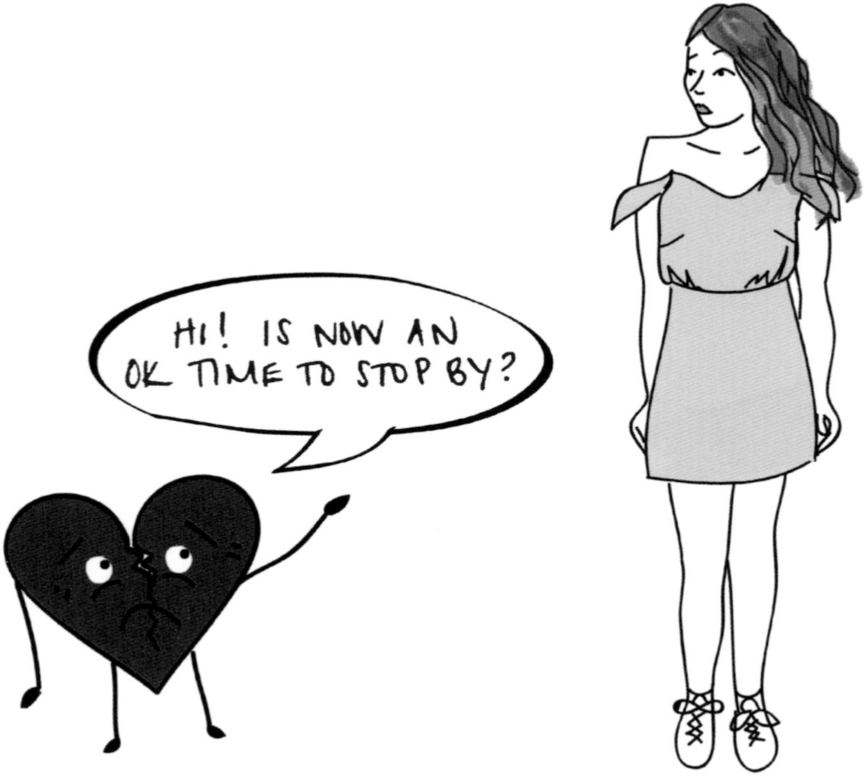
HI! IS NOW AN OK TIME TO STOP BY?

as good a time as ever.

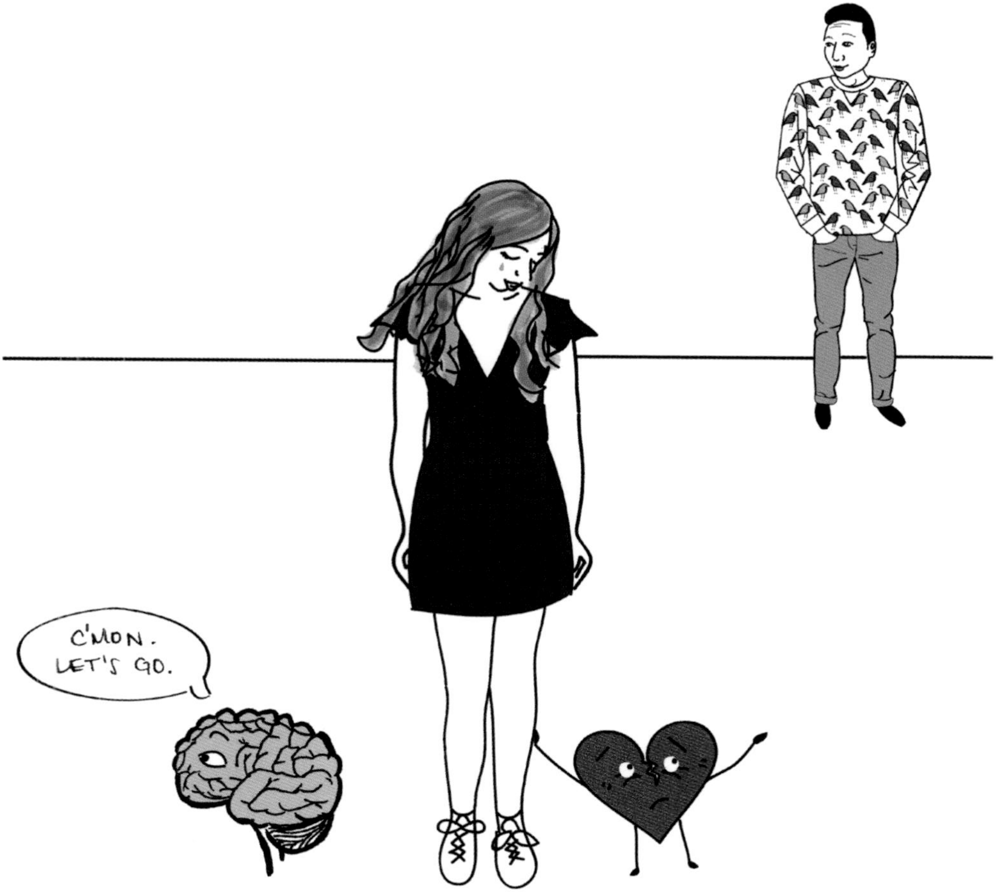
C'MON.
LET'S GO.

pulled in two directions.

when I'm trying to forget

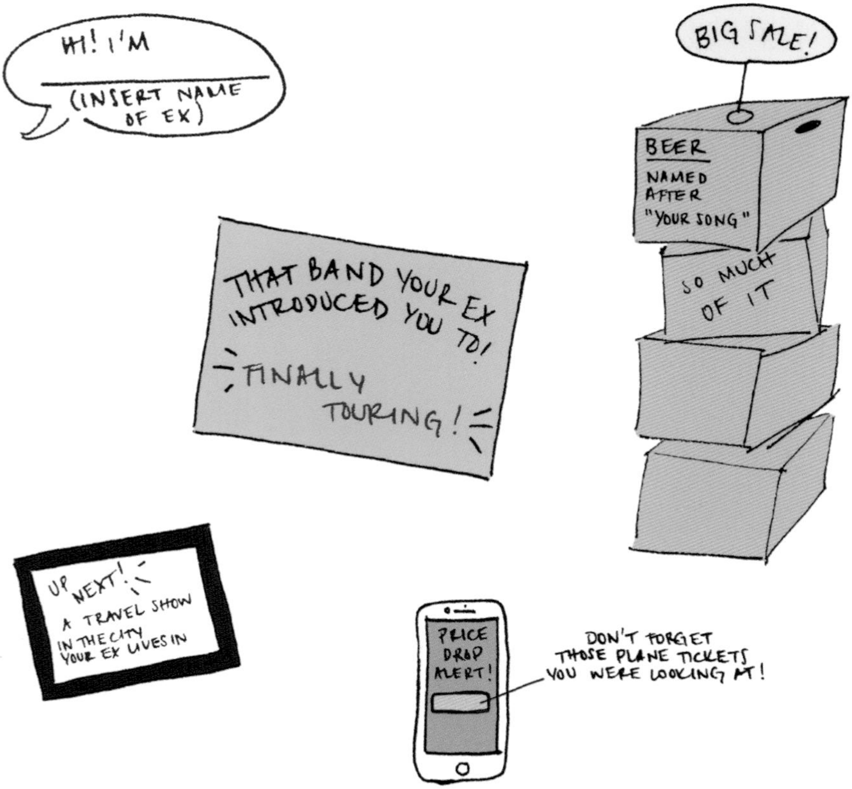
HI! I'M
(INSERT NAME OF EX)
BIG SALE!
BEER
NAMED AFTER "YOUR SONG"
SO MUCH OF IT
THAT BAND YOUR EX INTRODUCED YOU TO!
FINALLY TOURING!
UP NEXT!
A TRAVEL SHOW IN THE CITY YOUR EX LIVES IN
PRICE DROP ALERT!
DON'T FORGET THOSE PLANE TICKETS YOU WERE LOOKING AT!

little signs with big impacts.

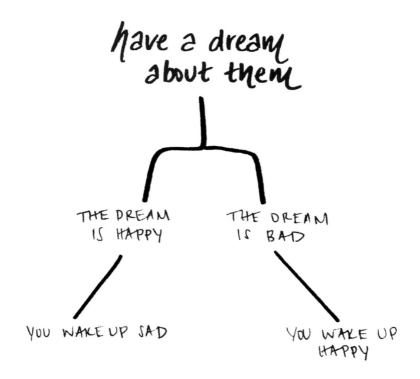

have a dream
about them

THE DREAM
IS HAPPY

THE DREAM
IS BAD

YOU WAKE UP SAD

YOU WAKE UP
HAPPY

a lose/lose.

THE HERO WAS THE VILLAIN ALL ALONG: THE HARDEST PART IS MOVING ON

I'm a fighter to the extreme and I love a challenge. It's impossible for me to back down from one; I thrive on them. Sometimes, though, there's nothing to be gained. With rejection comes struggle, and we've all felt that urge to fight even when the battle is long over, or to dwell defensively on moments that stung. But the good news is, this is the hardest part.

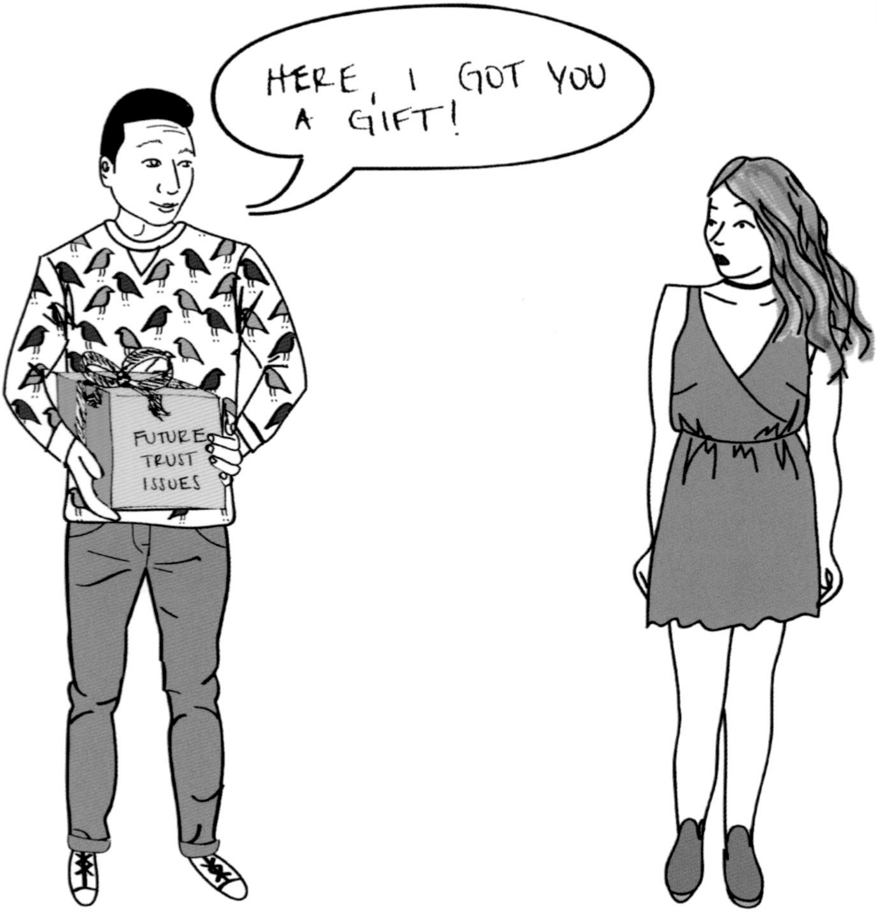
HERE, I GOT YOU A GIFT!
FUTURE TRUST ISSUES

the gift that keeps on giving.

aftereffects

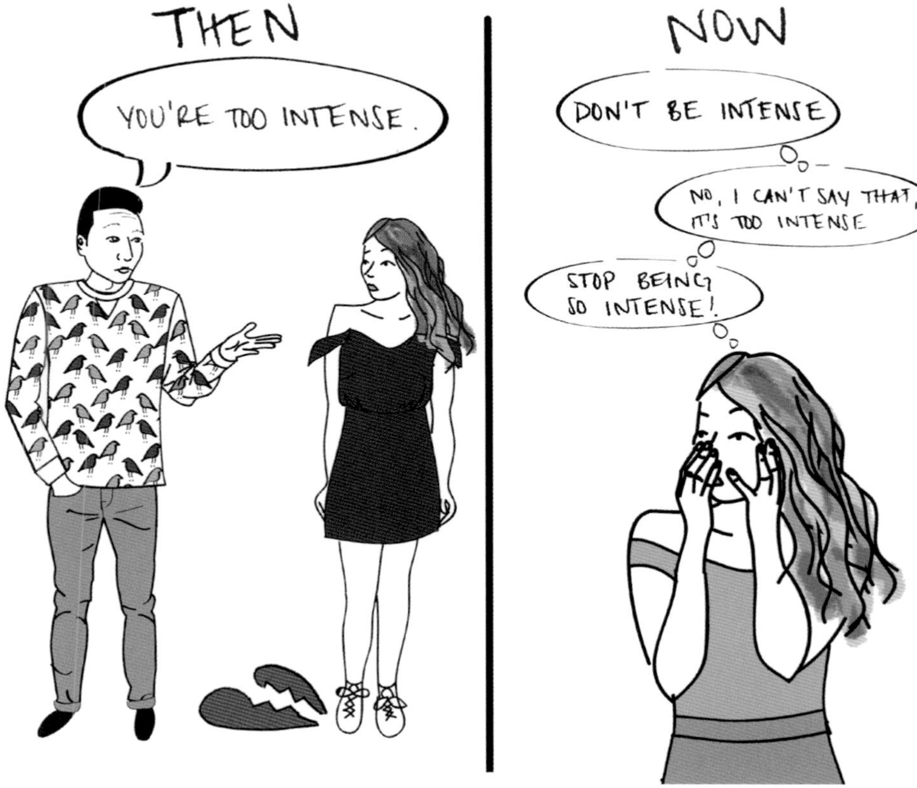

THEN
NOW
YOU'RE TOO INTENSE.
DON'T BE INTENSE
NO, I CAN'T SAY THAT, IT'S TOO INTENSE
STOP BEING SO INTENSE!

lovely remnants.

relationship café

<u>Prix fixe</u>

to start
Choice of one:

DISAPPOINTING SEX
PASSIONATE BUT SLOPPY KISS
DIRTY MIRROR NUDES

mains
Choice of one:

LISTENING TO COMPLAINTS ABOUT EX
LISTENING TO COMPLAINTS ABOUT CAREER
LISTENING TO ENDLESS HUMBLE BRAGS

sweet endings
Choice of one:

UNRECIPROCATED VULNERABILITY
NEVER SPEAKING AGAIN

I'll have the buffet. you?

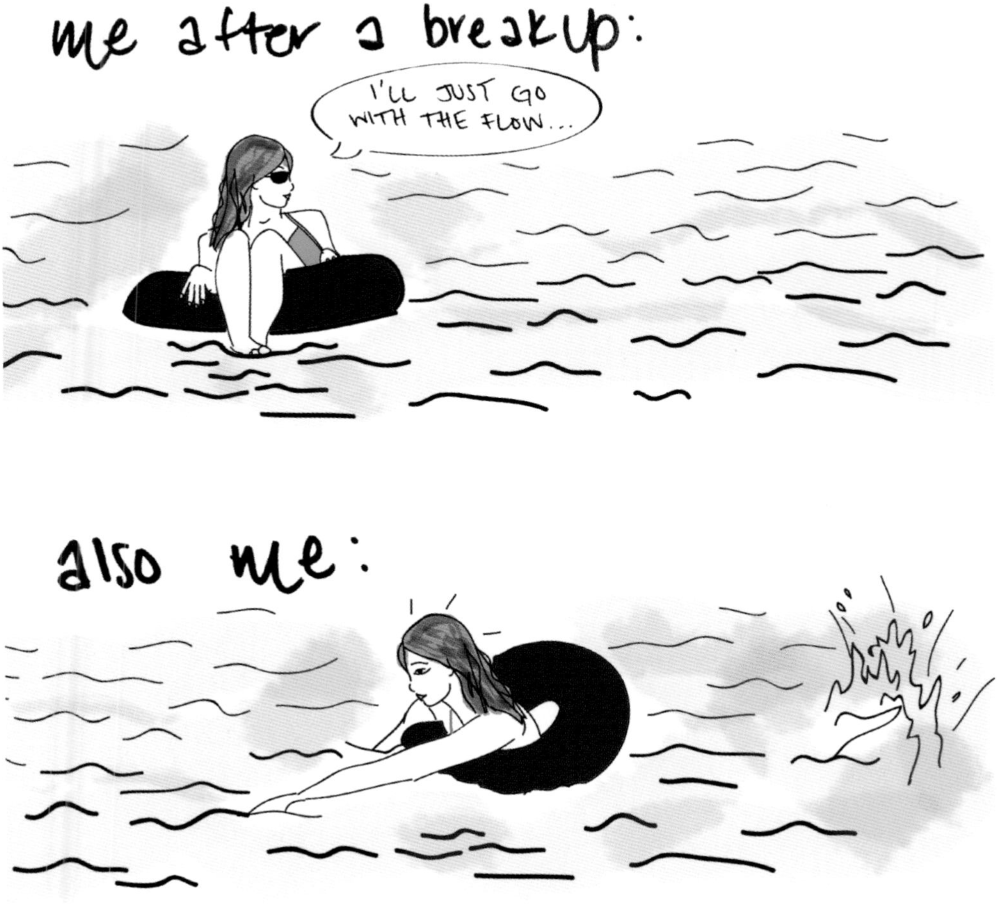
me after a breakup:
I'LL JUST GO WITH THE FLOW...
also me:

but let's be real—it's mostly the bottom one.

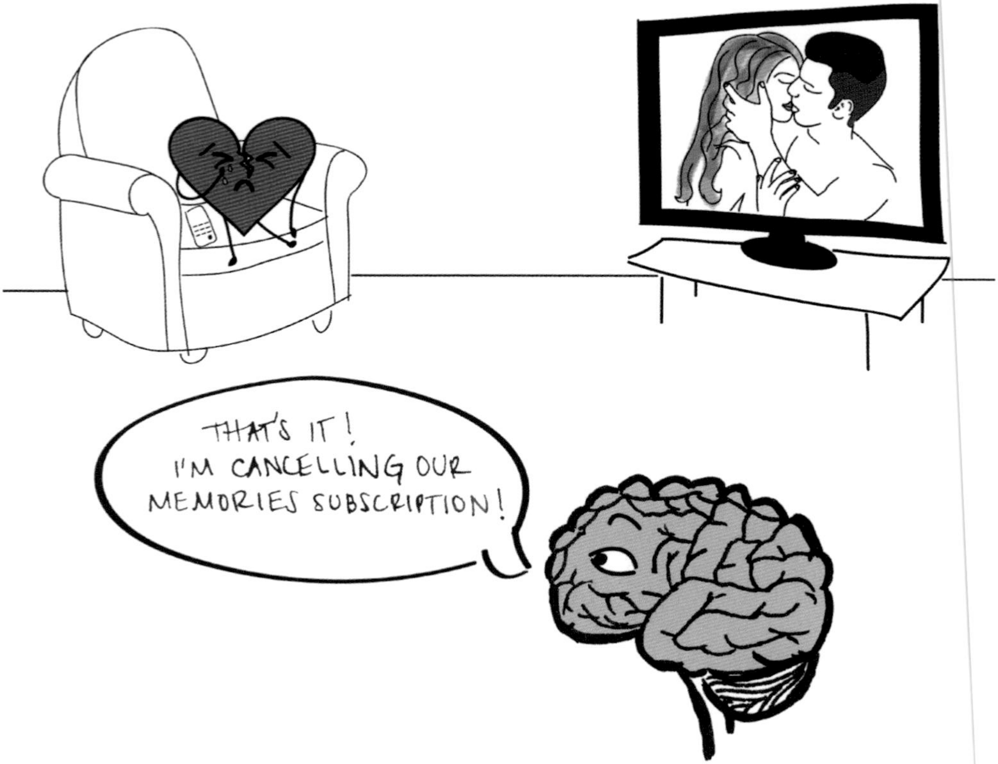
THAT'S IT!
I'M CANCELLING OUR MEMORIES SUBSCRIPTION!

stop hitting rewind.

it feels different

every single time

it heals differently, too.

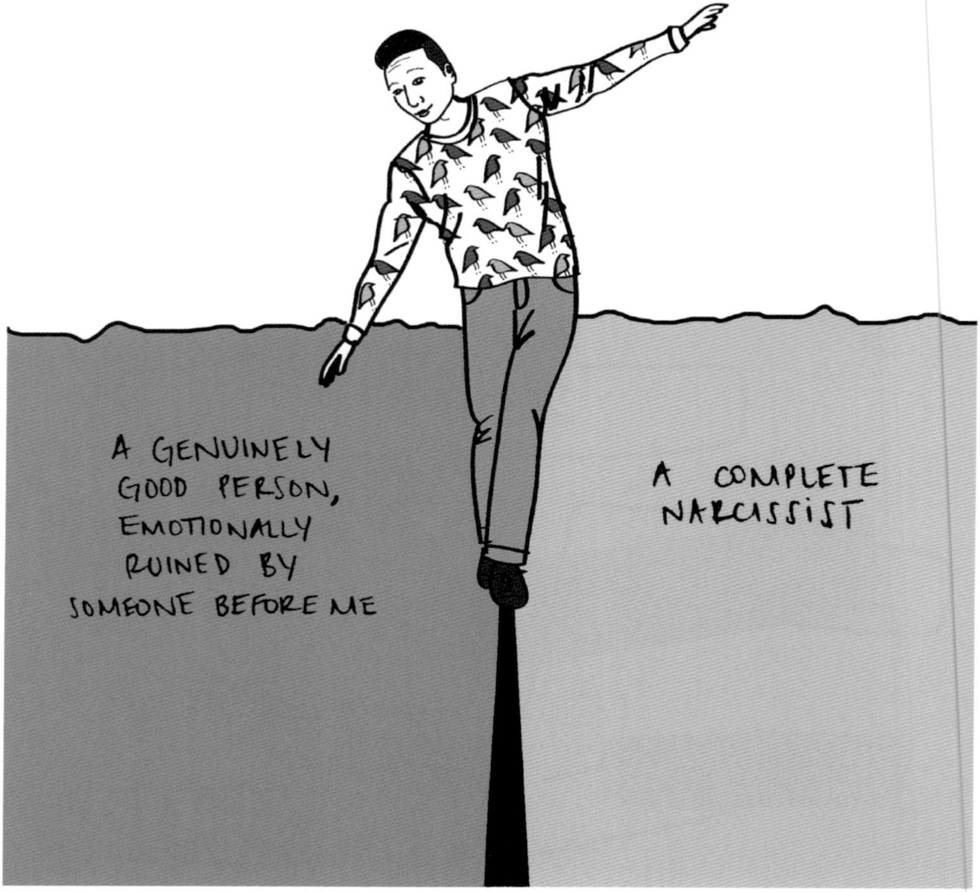
A GENUINELY GOOD PERSON, EMOTIONALLY RUINED BY SOMEONE BEFORE ME
A COMPLETE NARCISSIST

it's a very, very fine line.

currently

MENTALLY GIVING UP HOPE
TO LOWER MY EXPECTATIONS
AND AVOID FUTURE
DISAPPOINTMENT
FROM YOU
DESPERATELY
KEEPING MY HEART
OPEN JUST IN CASE

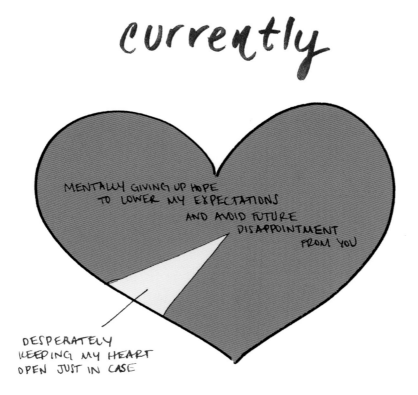

I guess it is possible to have it all?

REMEMBER SOMETHING NICE THEY DID
REMINISCE
REMEMBER SOMETHING SHITTY THEY DID
SEETHE

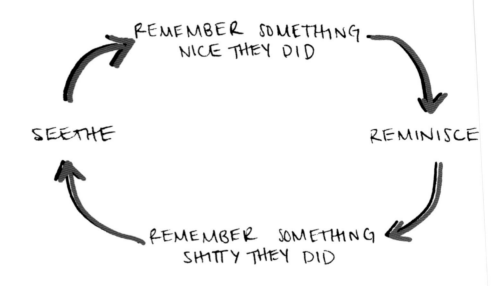

a seemingly endless loop.

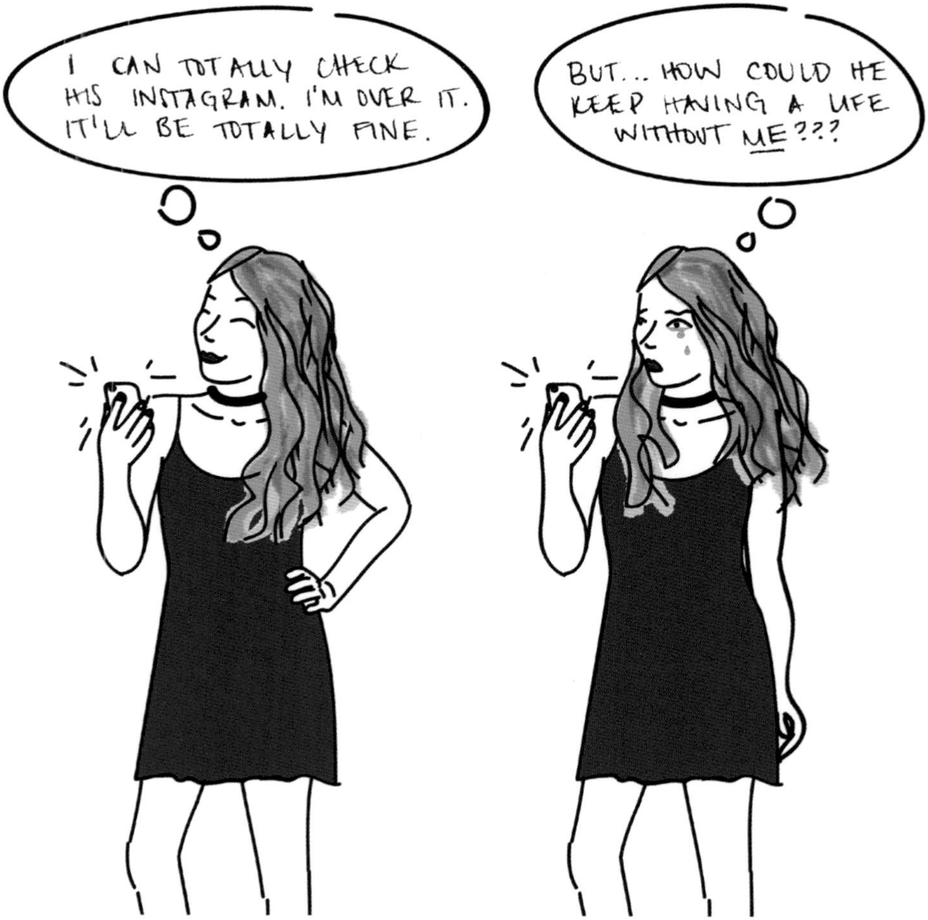
I CAN TOTALLY CHECK HIS INSTAGRAM. I'M OVER IT. IT'LL BE TOTALLY FINE.
BUT... HOW COULD HE KEEP HAVING A LIFE WITHOUT ME???

he still exists??

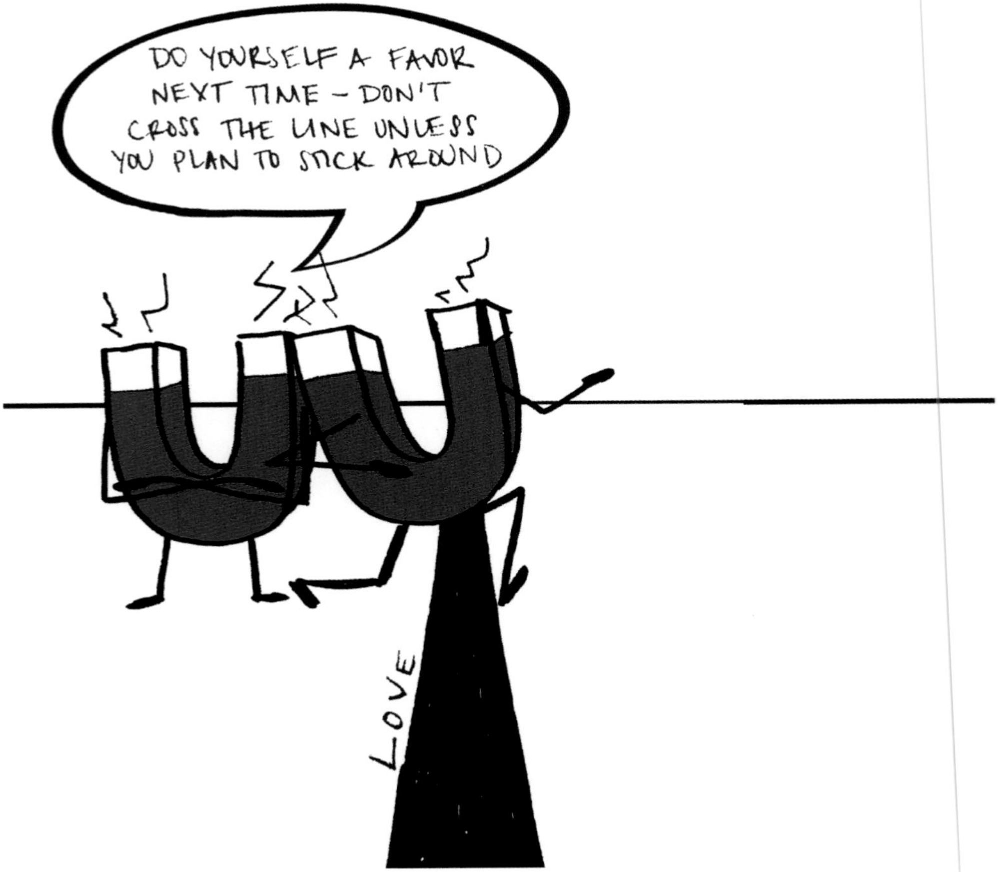
DO YOURSELF A FAVOR NEXT TIME - DON'T CROSS THE LINE UNLESS YOU PLAN TO STICK AROUND
LOVE

you were dangerously attractive.

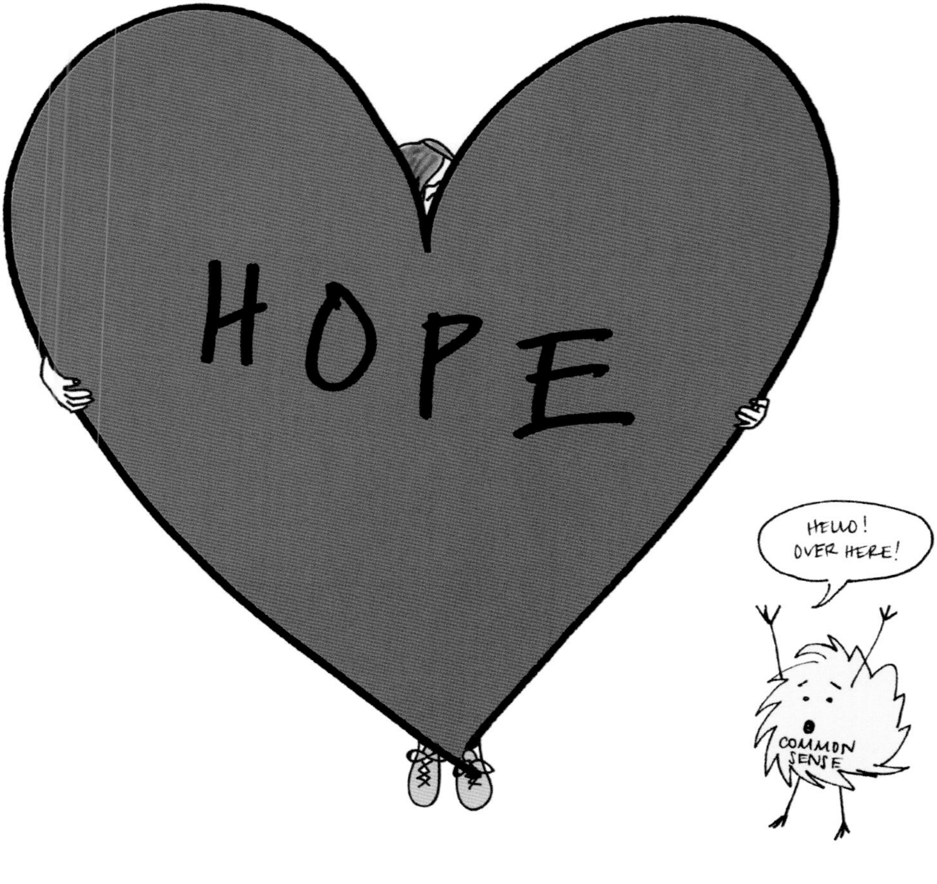
HOPE
HELLO! OVER HERE!
COMMON SENSE

out of sight, out of mind.

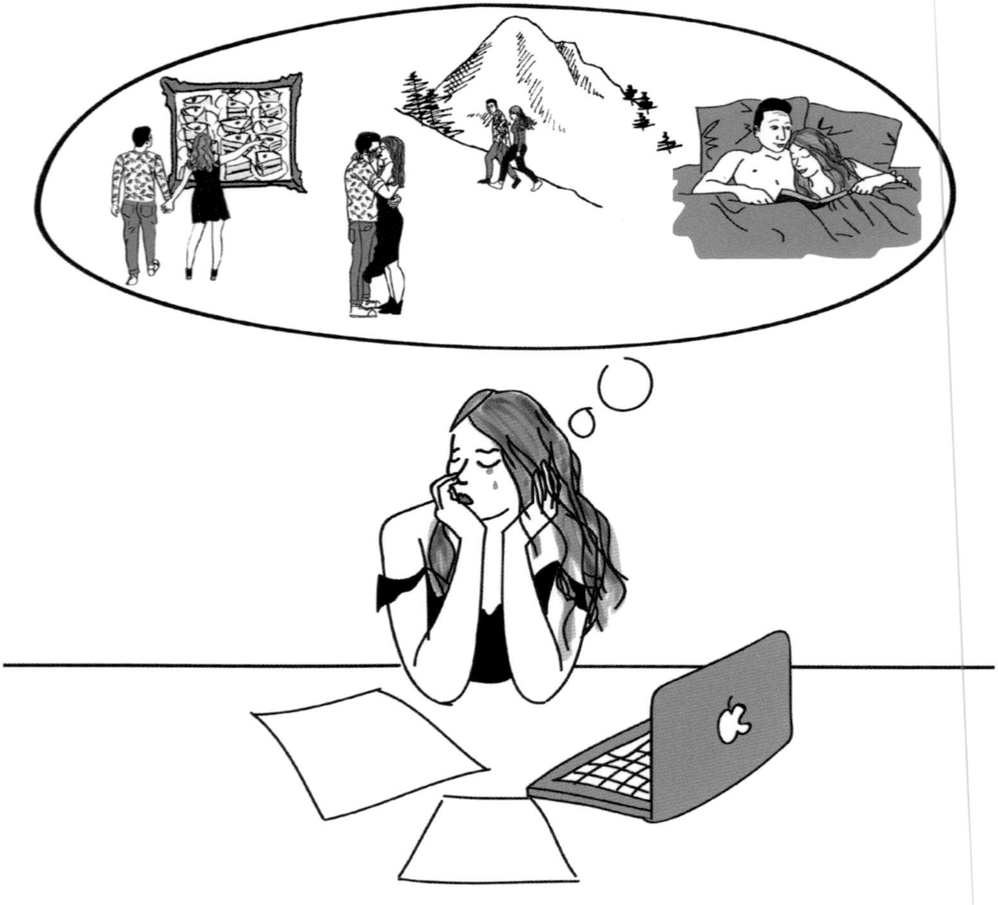

they're still in my head.

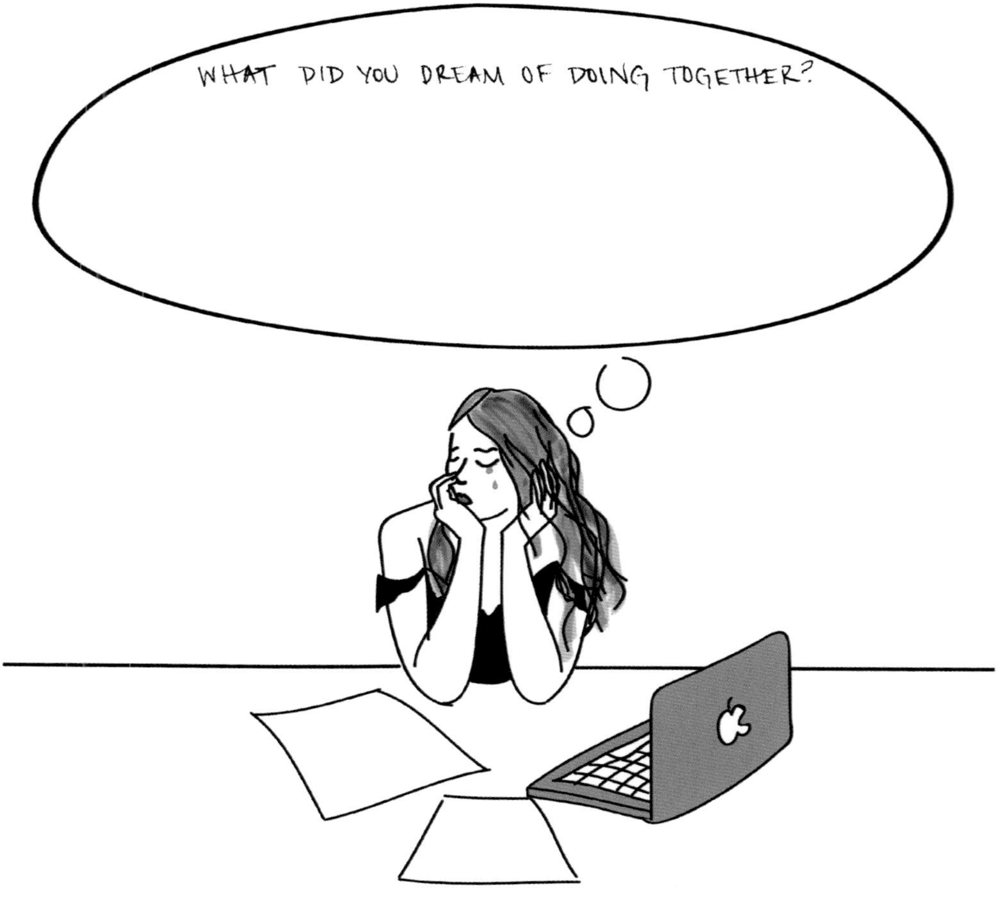
WHAT DID YOU DREAM OF DOING TOGETHER?

how it was

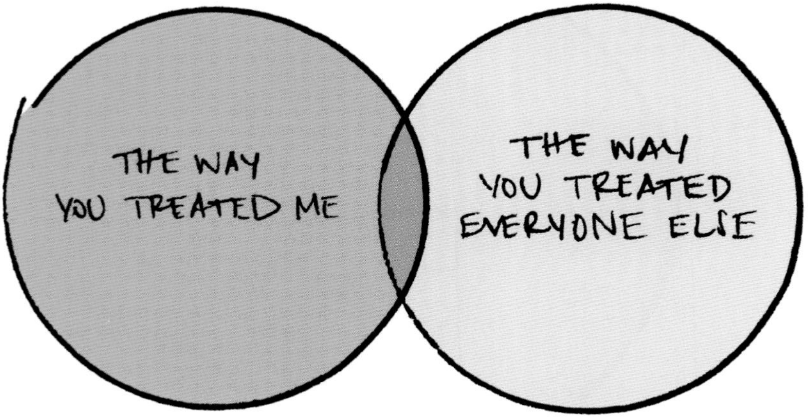
THE WAY YOU TREATED ME
THE WAY YOU TREATED EVERYONE ELSE

how it is

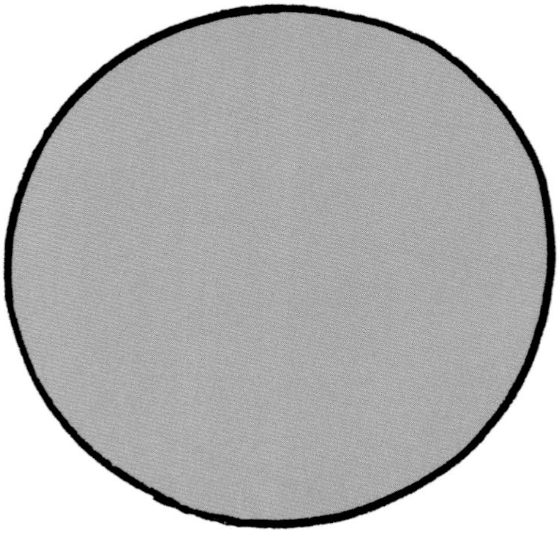

and how it's going to be.

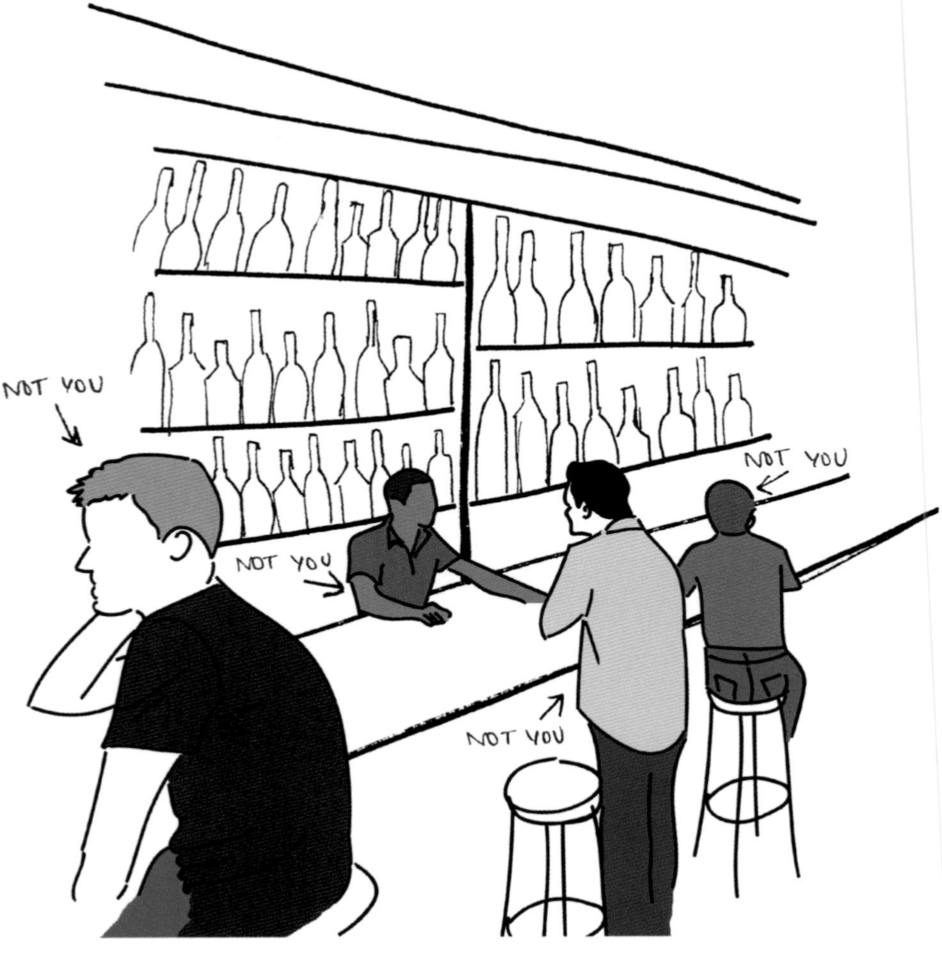
NOT YOU
NOT YOU
NOT YOU
NOT YOU

don't care, don't care, don't care.

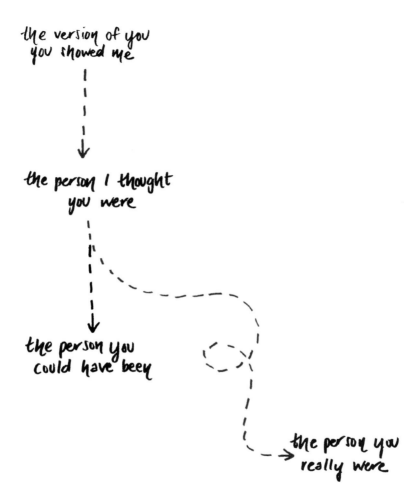

the version of you
you showed me

the person I thought
you were

the person you
could have been

the person you
really were

detour.

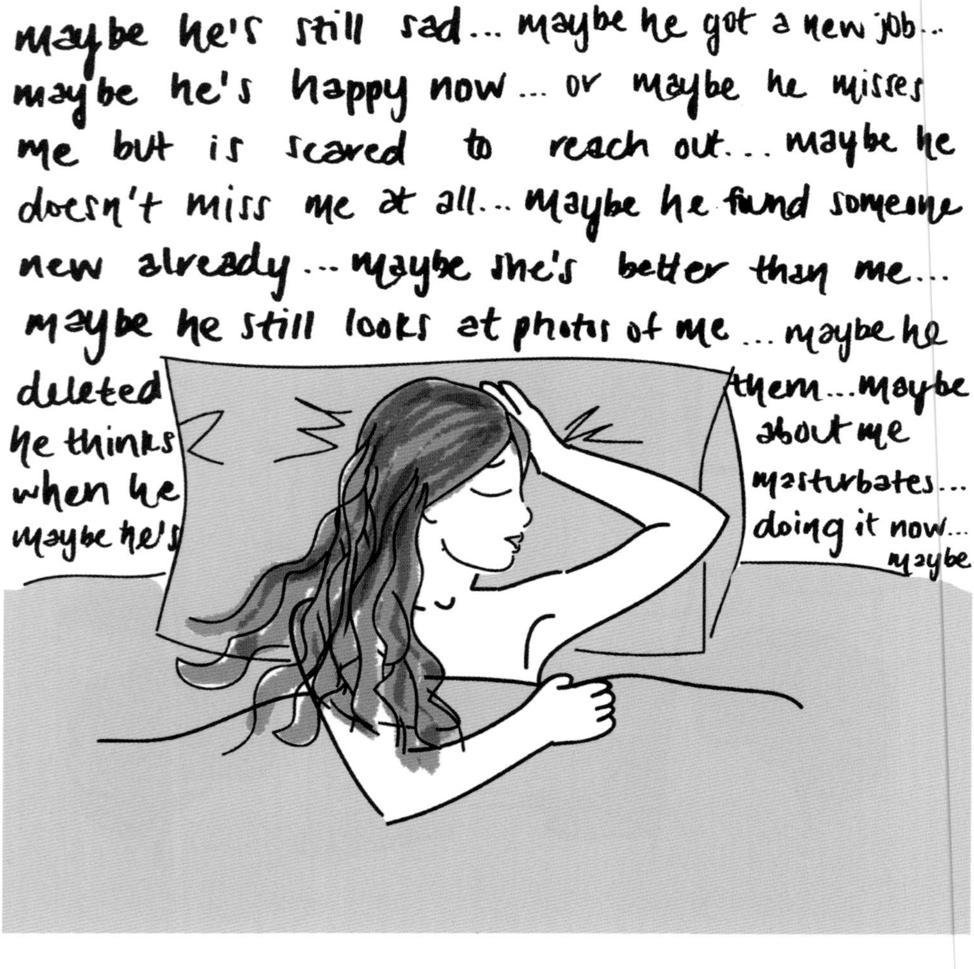
maybe he's still sad... maybe he got a new job...
maybe he's happy now... or maybe he misses
me but is scared to reach out... maybe he
doesn't miss me at all... maybe he found someone
new already... maybe she's better than me...
maybe he still looks at photos of me... maybe he
deleted them... maybe
he thinks about me
when he masturbates...
maybe he's doing it now...
maybe

the opposite of counting sheep.

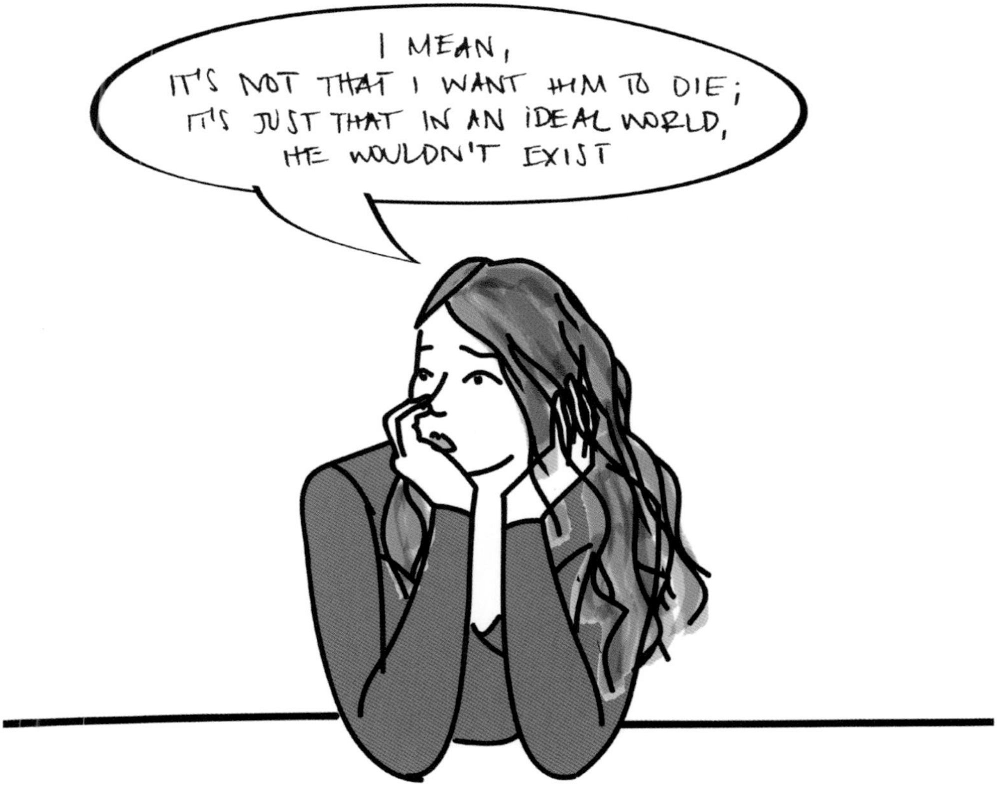
I MEAN,
IT'S NOT THAT I WANT HIM TO DIE;
IT'S JUST THAT IN AN IDEAL WORLD,
HE WOULDN'T EXIST

and I've always been an idealist.

A Respite, Finally: Let Go, and You Will Begin to Feel Free

No one wants to suffer forever. Possibly the most annoying thing someone can say to you during a time of grief is, "Time heals all wounds." What's worse is that this adage is indisputably true. After you've stopped (for the most part) fighting the current, things start to flow a bit more smoothly. Moving on isn't easy, but a bit of perspective always helps.

a study of perspective:

THEN:
NOW:
heartbreaker
My bedroom
HE'S SUCH A FOODIE, I LOVE IT
I LOVE HIS COMPOSITION; HE HAS SUCH A GREAT EYE
OMG, I LOVE THAT BOOK! HE IS SO INTELLECTUAL
THERE'S DEFINITELY SOMETHING SEXY ABOUT A MAN DRINKING AN ARTISANAL CAPPUCCINO
I HOPE THIS CROISSANT GOES STRAIGHT TO HIS BELLY
OVERALL TRYING WAY TOO HARD TO BE HIPSTER
GOD HE IS SO PRETENTIOUS, NO ONE CARES WHAT BOOK YOU'RE READING
HE ORDERED THIS JUST SO HE COULD TAKE A COOL PHOTO

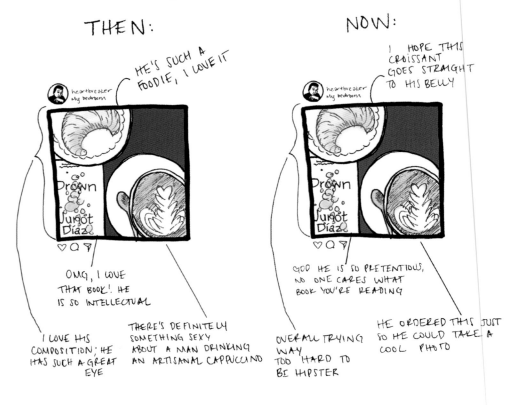

the beauty of social media.

your turn

DRAW SOMETHING
ABOUT YOUR EX THAT YOU NOW
HAVE A DIFFERENT PERSPECTIVE ON

THEN :   NOW :

how to get over a breakup

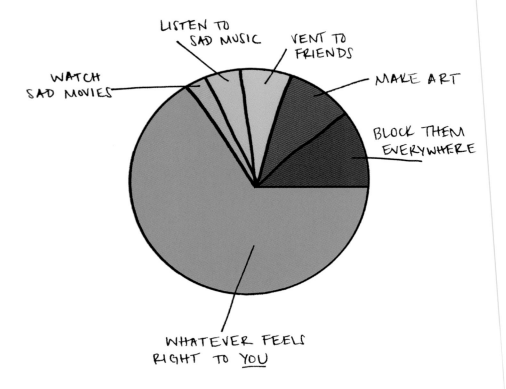

LISTEN TO
SAD MUSIC

VENT TO
FRIENDS

WATCH
SAD MOVIES

MAKE ART

BLOCK THEM
EVERYWHERE

WHATEVER FEELS
RIGHT TO YOU

you do you, and don't let anyone tell you otherwise.

ideal qualities

- ☑ APPRECIATES CREATIVITY
- ☑ ADVENTUROUS AND OPEN-MINDED
- ☑ MOTIVATED AND AMBITIOUS
- ☑ PASSIONATE
- ☑ INDEPENDENT
- ☑ AFFECTIONATE
- ☐ WANTS ME UNCONDITIONALLY

you couldn't check the most important box.

red flags I ignored

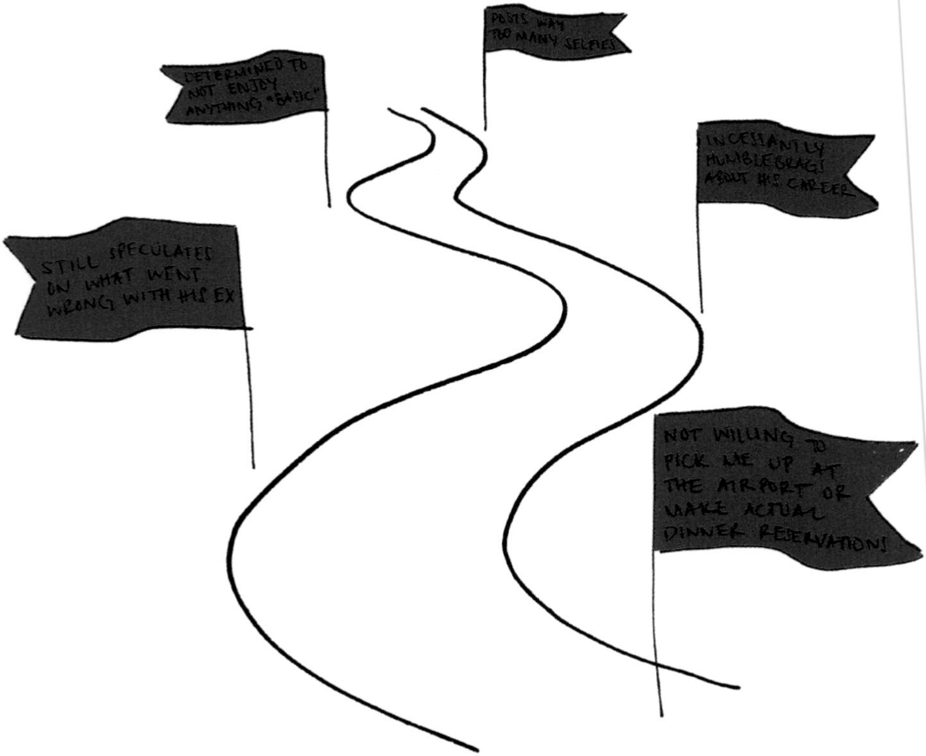
POSTS WAY TOO MANY SELFIES
DETERMINED TO NOT ENJOY ANYTHING "BASIC"
INCESSANTLY HUMBLEBRAGS ABOUT HIS CAREER
STILL SPECULATES ON WHAT WENT WRONG WITH HIS EX
NOT WILLING TO PICK ME UP AT THE AIRPORT OR MAKE ACTUAL DINNER RESERVATIONS

were those really always there?

what did you ignore?

progress

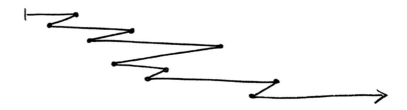

three steps forward, two steps back.

today I feel:

A. LIKE I SAW YOU JUST YESTERDAY

B. LIKE I HAVEN'T SEEN YOU IN
   A MILLION YEARS

C. LIKE I WISH I COULD SEE YOU

D. LIKE I NEVER WANT TO SEE YOU AGAIN

E. ALL OF THE ABOVE

what is time, anyway?

I now have the time + courage
to try that thing that

I never had the time or courage
to try before

and it feels so good.

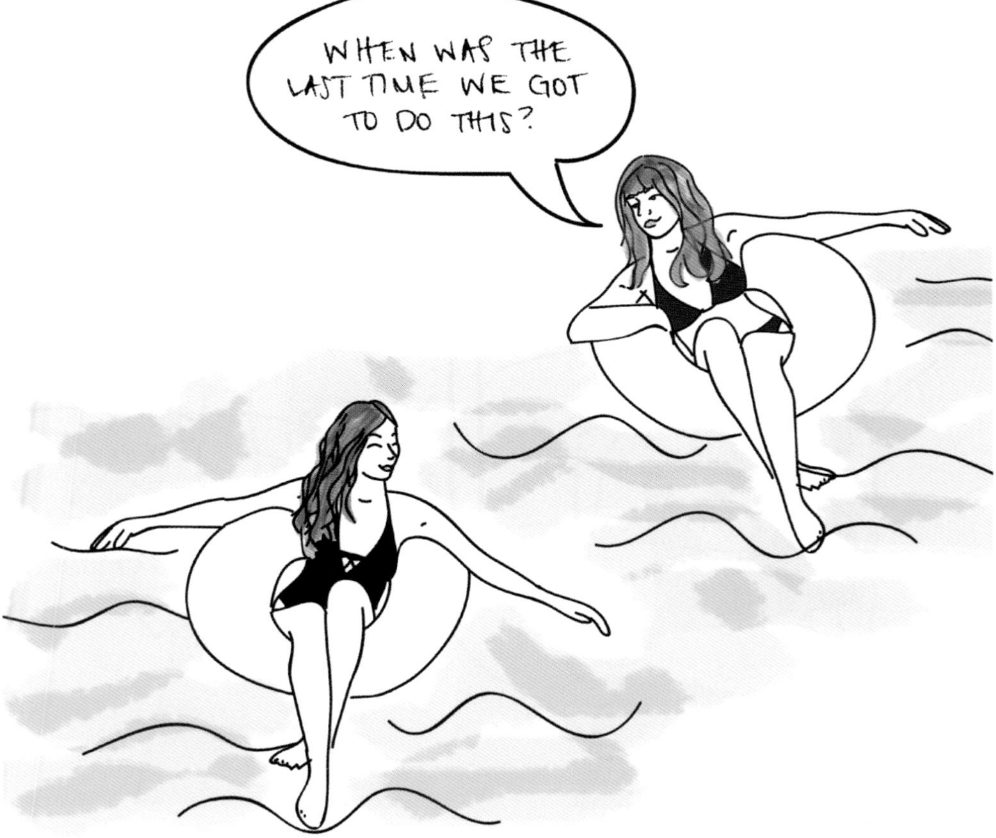
WHEN WAS THE LAST TIME WE GOT TO DO THIS?

things are calmer now that you're gone.

some days
it feels like this

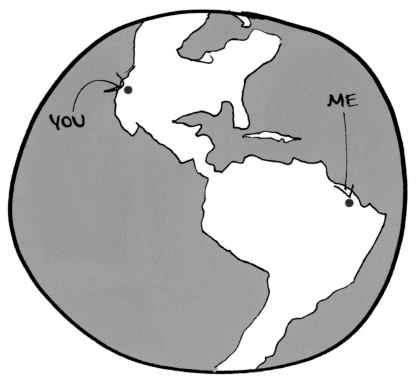

so far . . .

other days
it feels like this

and yet, so close.

expectation

MY HEART WILL HURT
THIS BADLY FOREVER

I'LL ALWAYS WANT
TO TALK TO YOU ONE
LAST TIME

EVENTUALLY I'LL FEEL
NOTHING FOR YOU

reality

I ALREADY FEEL
BETTER

I DON'T NEED TO
HEAR FROM YOU
ANYMORE

YOU WILL ALWAYS HAVE
A PIECE OF MY SOUL,
AND THAT'S OK

baby steps.

what were yours?

expectation   reality

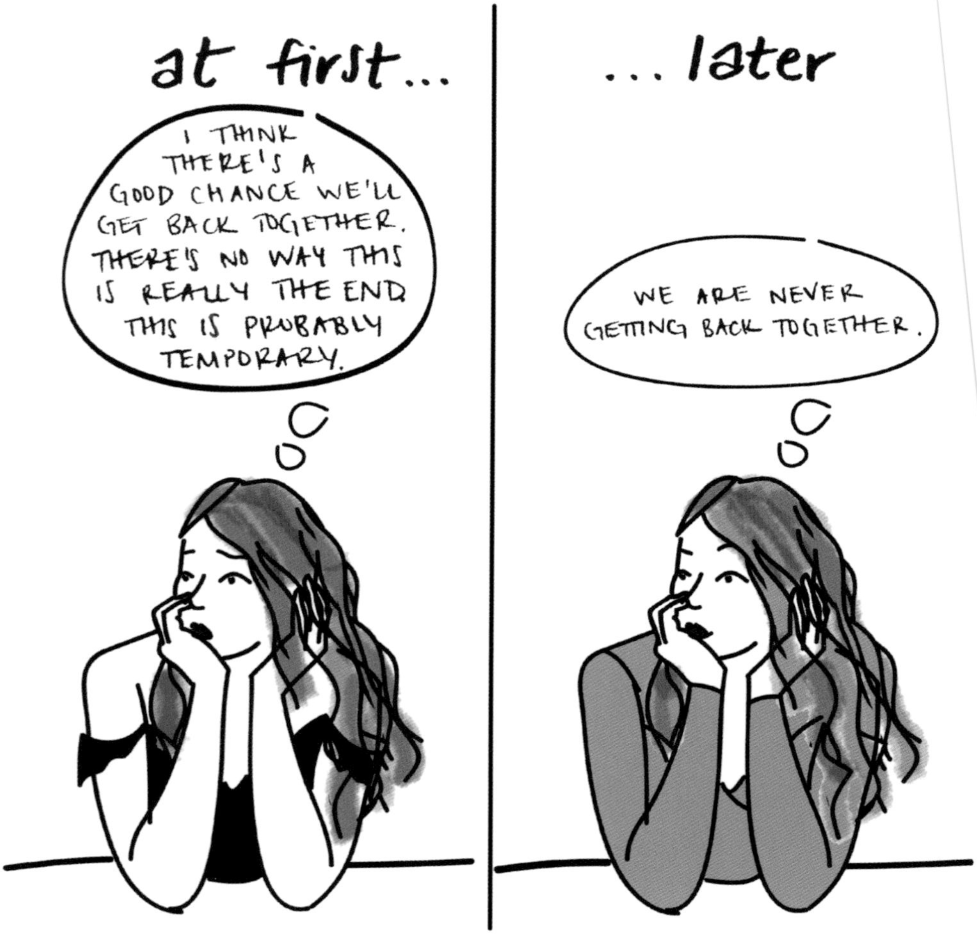
at first...
I THINK THERE'S A GOOD CHANCE WE'LL GET BACK TOGETHER. THERE'S NO WAY THIS IS REALLY THE END. THIS IS PROBABLY TEMPORARY.
...later
WE ARE NEVER GETTING BACK TOGETHER.

time, you tricky friend.

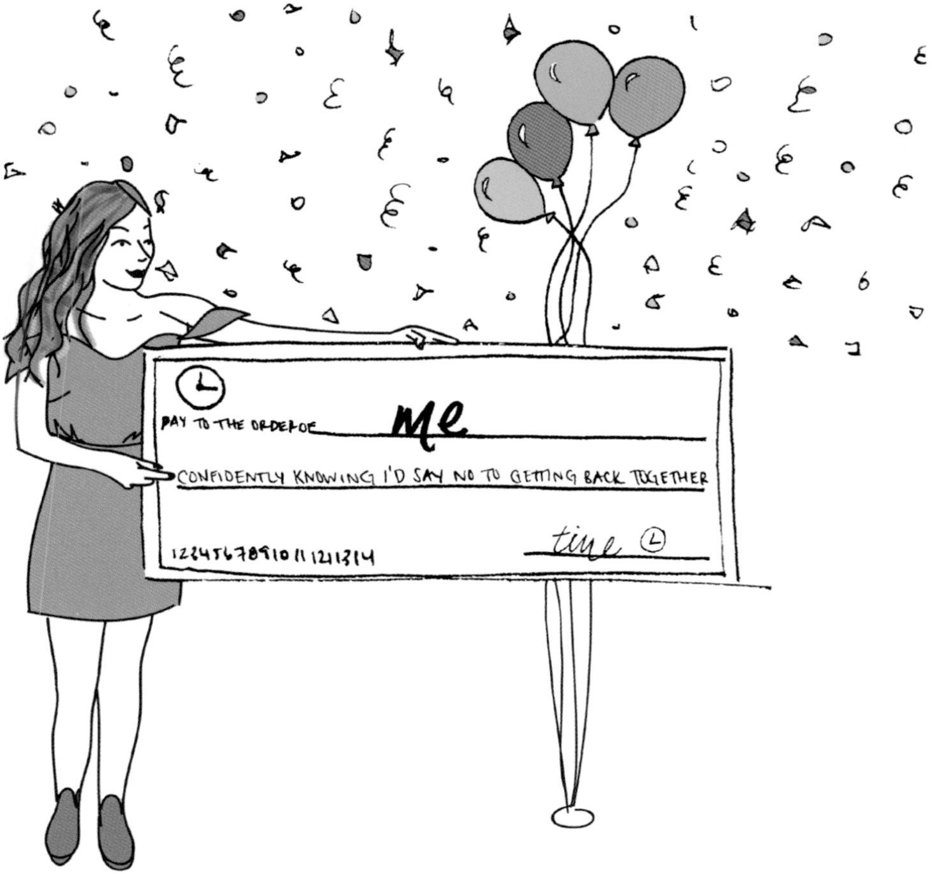
PAY TO THE ORDER OF me
CONFIDENTLY KNOWING I'D SAY NO TO GETTING BACK TOGETHER
time

true wealth.

JUST BECAUSE IT'S GONE, DOESN'T MEAN IT'S GONE: IT'S OK TO LOOK BACK

We all have days when a scent in the air or music on our playlist suddenly transports us back and triggers strong memories. It might be a specific cologne, the song you heard at the bar on your first date, or an artist you both loved. For me, it's the smell of bourbon, "Samson" by Regina Spektor, and painter Wayne Thiebaud. These associations won't always be painful, I promise. For now, though, feel them, acknowledge them, and let them slowly fade.

every once in a while

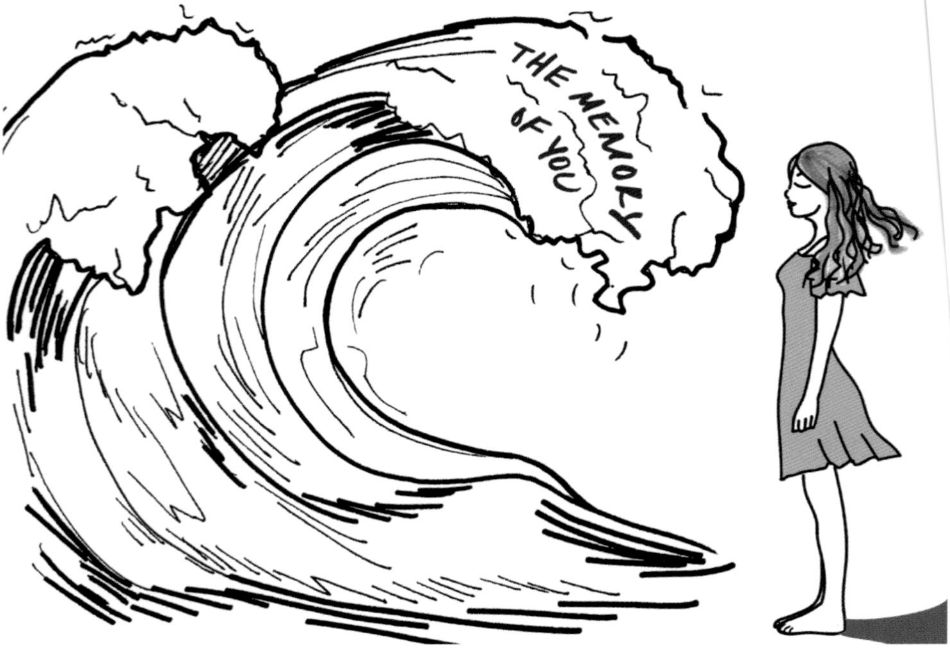
THE MEMORY
OF YOU

and that's ok.

the things you were

PLAYLIST COLLABORATOR

Here's a playlist for you...
Feb mix 2 - 2017

OW

Feb mix 2 - 2017 a playlist by Birdshirt on Spotify

HAIR DETANGLER

HARMONIZER

I Love you, al - ways for-ev-er

BOOK RECOMMENDER

the RICE MOTHER
DROWN   Junot Díaz
The Remains of the Day

POETIC COMPLIMENTER

I LOVE YOUR FULL LIPS AND YOUR GREEN EYES AND YOUR FRECKLED NOSE. YOU ARE SO RADIANT.

I guess I'd better buy myself a hairbrush.

all of a sudden...

I MISS THE SCAR
ON THE BACK
OF YOUR HEAD

among other little things.

Selective memory

= MOMENTS I REMEMBER
LEVEL OF HAPPINESS
LENGTH OF RELATIONSHIP

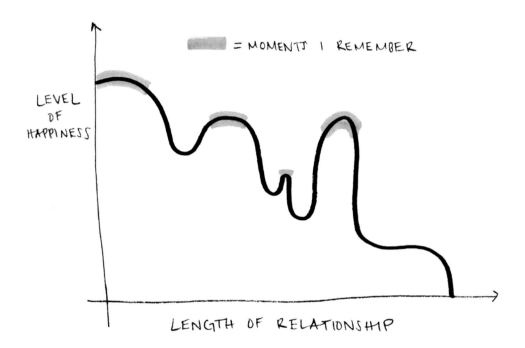

those dips never happened, right?

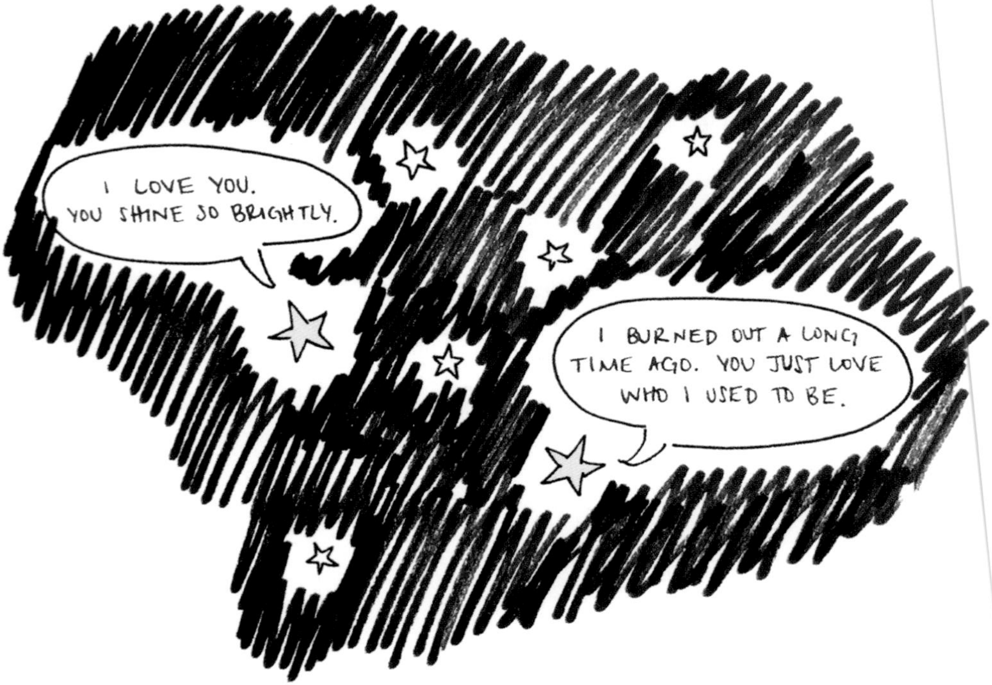
I LOVE YOU.
YOU SHINE SO BRIGHTLY.
I BURNED OUT A LONG TIME AGO. YOU JUST LOVE WHO I USED TO BE.

you were always brilliant to me.

you left
a mark
I don't want
to erase

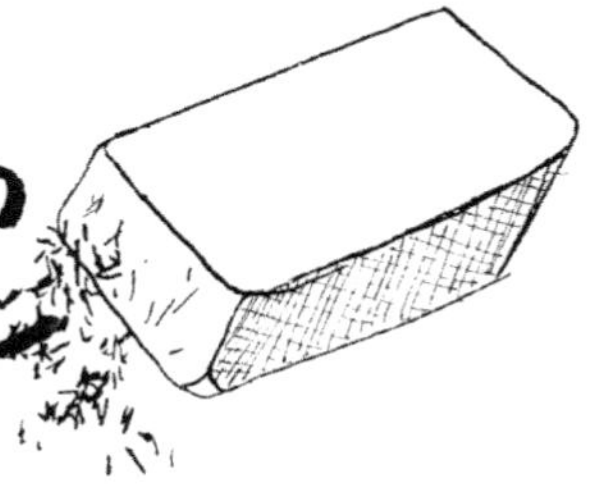

I'll keep the good parts.

things you made me question

IS BAD SEX REALLY BETTER
  THAN NO SEX?

CAN A PERSON REALLY BE
  THAT NUMB?

CAN YOU BE SIMULTANEOUSLY
  CONFIDENT AND INSECURE?

IS IT ME?

IS IT YOU?

WHAT IF I HAD DONE THAT
  ONE THING DIFFERENTLY?

what were your
   unanswered questions?

DO THEY MATTER?

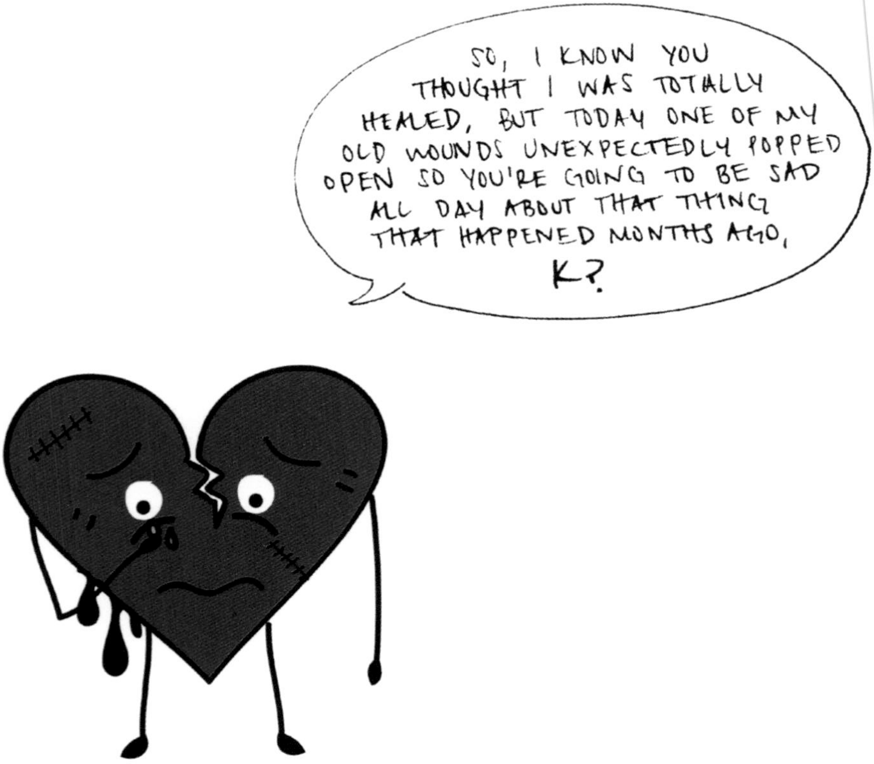
SO, I KNOW YOU THOUGHT I WAS TOTALLY HEALED, BUT TODAY ONE OF MY OLD WOUNDS UNEXPECTEDLY POPPED OPEN SO YOU'RE GOING TO BE SAD ALL DAY ABOUT THAT THING THAT HAPPENED MONTHS AGO, K?

surprise!

should I text my ex?

DO YOU STILL TALK?
NO
YES
WILL YOU BE UPSET IF THEY DON'T RESPOND?
DO YOU FEEL OK ABOUT THAT?
NO
YES
NO
YES
WILL YOU FEEL BETTER AFTER GETTING IT OFF YOUR CHEST?
DON'T TEXT
TELL ME YOUR SECRET
NO
YES
ARE YOU SURE?
NO
YES
TEXT AT YOUR OWN RISK!

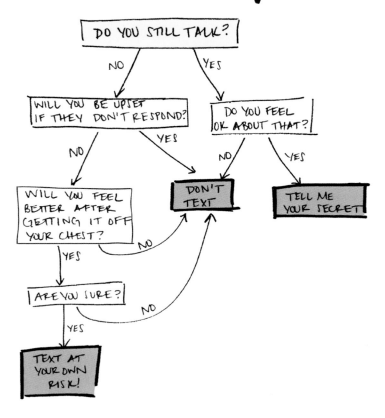

but really, it's probably never a good idea.

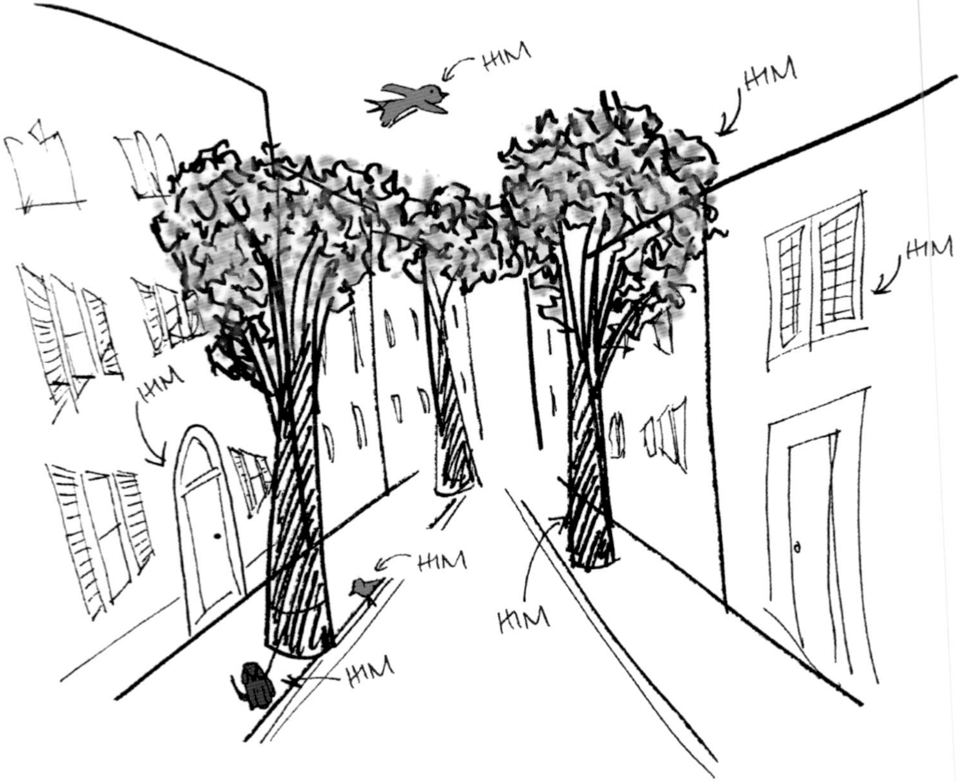
HIM
HIM
HIM
HIM
HIM
HIM
HIM

those days when everything is a reminder.

you will never be

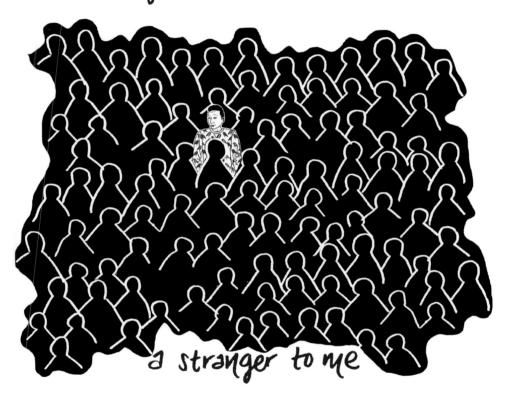

a stranger to me

my soul will always recognize yours.

a timeline

I WAS HAPPY	YOU HURT ME	I CAN STILL BE HAPPY

you were just a little blip.

BEAUTIFUL
STILL BEAUTIFUL

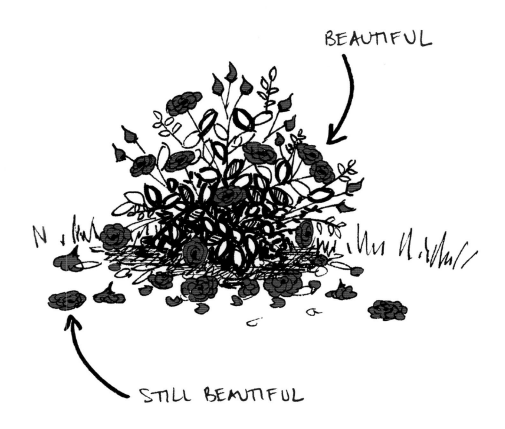

just because something ends
doesn't mean it wasn't good.

gifts that you gave me

AN APPRECIATION FOR YOUR INTERESTS, SOME OF WHICH BECAME MINE
EVEN MORE CONFIDENCE IN MYSELF AND WHAT I DESERVE
HIGHER STANDARDS
POWER IN MY ABILITY TO HEAL
FEELING SEXY WHILE DOING MUNDANE ACTIVITIES

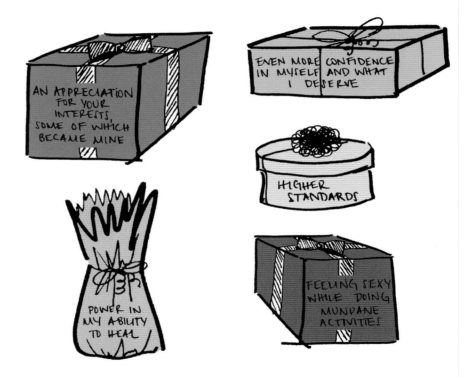

I'll take these with me.

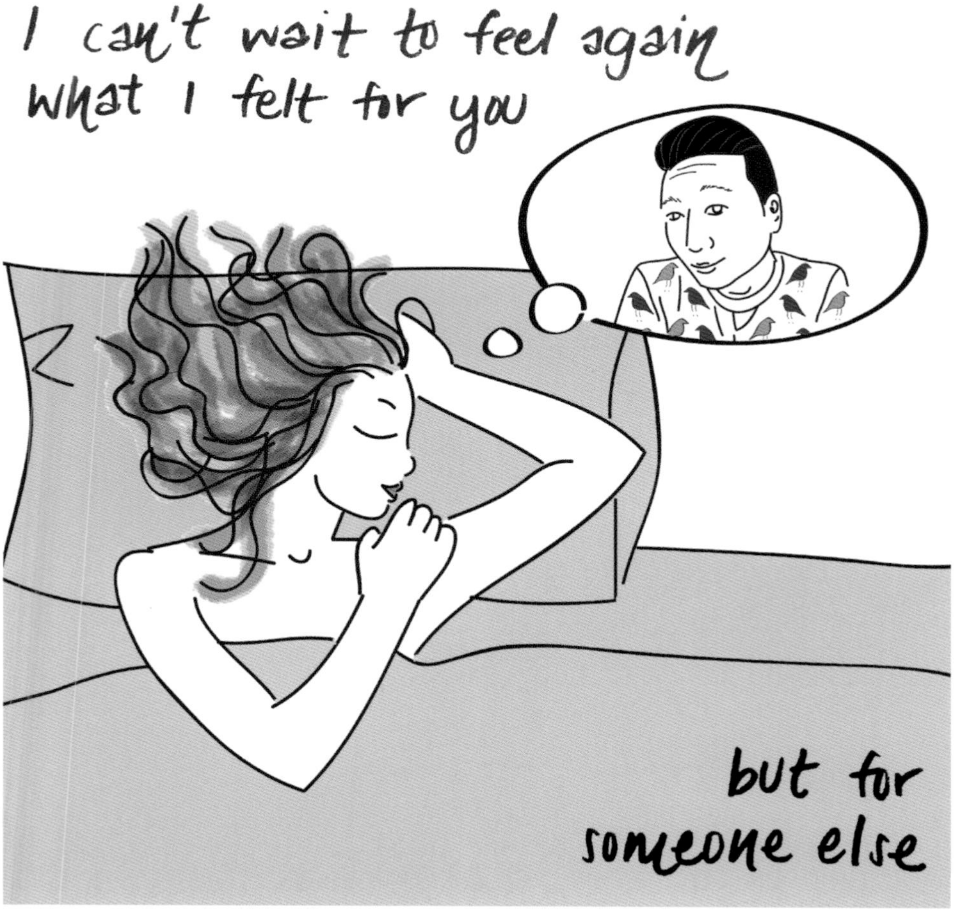
I can't wait to feel again what I felt for you
but for someone else

it feels different

every single time

same intensity, different spark.

places you can be:

= YES

= NO

I am only mine, now.

the kind things you said
are tattooed on my heart

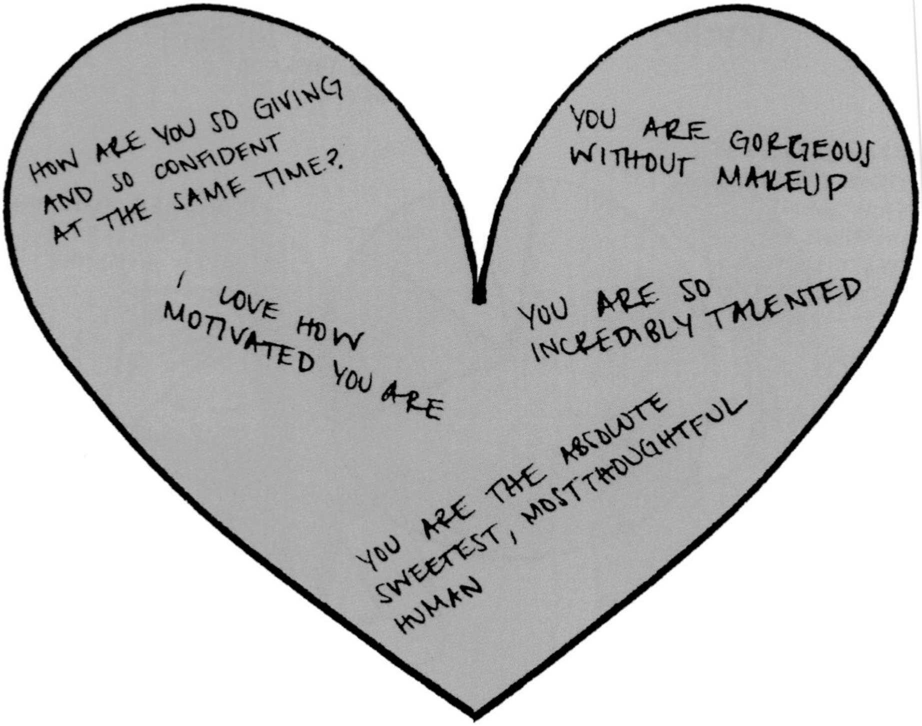
HOW ARE YOU SO GIVING AND SO CONFIDENT AT THE SAME TIME?
YOU ARE GORGEOUS WITHOUT MAKEUP
I LOVE HOW MOTIVATED YOU ARE
YOU ARE SO INCREDIBLY TALENTED
YOU ARE THE ABSOLUTE SWEETEST, MOST THOUGHTFUL HUMAN

it's all still true.

WRITE IN YOUR OWN!

THEIR WORDS ARE STILL HERE,
EVEN IF THEY'RE GONE

BECAUSE OF YOU, IN SPITE OF YOU: RESILIENCE GOT YOU HERE, EMPATHY WILL PUSH YOU FORWARD

Strength comes from struggle, and as you know by now, I've certainly struggled. I've found that the most powerful catalyst for getting over heartbreak is to channel that struggle into productivity. Learn to play guitar. Take up boxing. Start drawing. Write a book. There is no sweeter vindication than turning a rough situation into a rewarding one.

Maybe they couldn't love you the way you deserved, but you may love yourself more when it's all over.

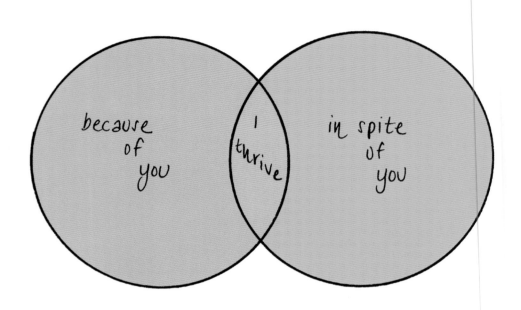

because of you

I thrive

in spite of you

it can't be both, but I still get all the credit.

fill in your own

reasons they were
bad for me:

reasons they were
good for me:

I learned a lesson

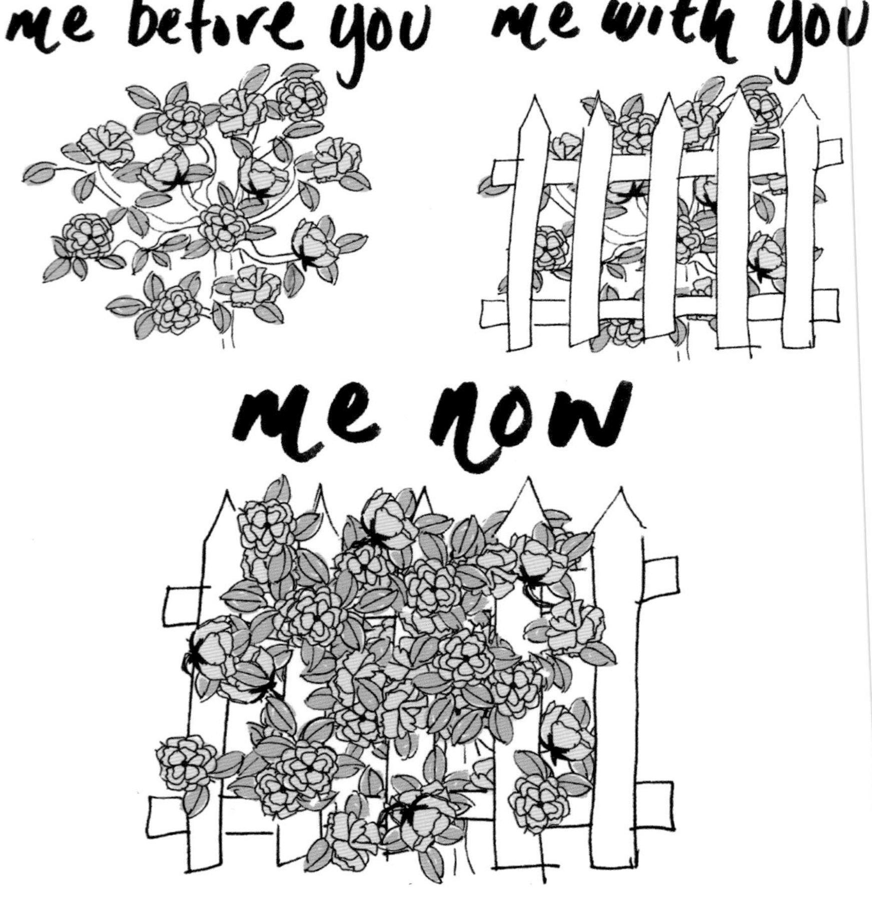
me before you
me with you
me now

you can't fence me in.

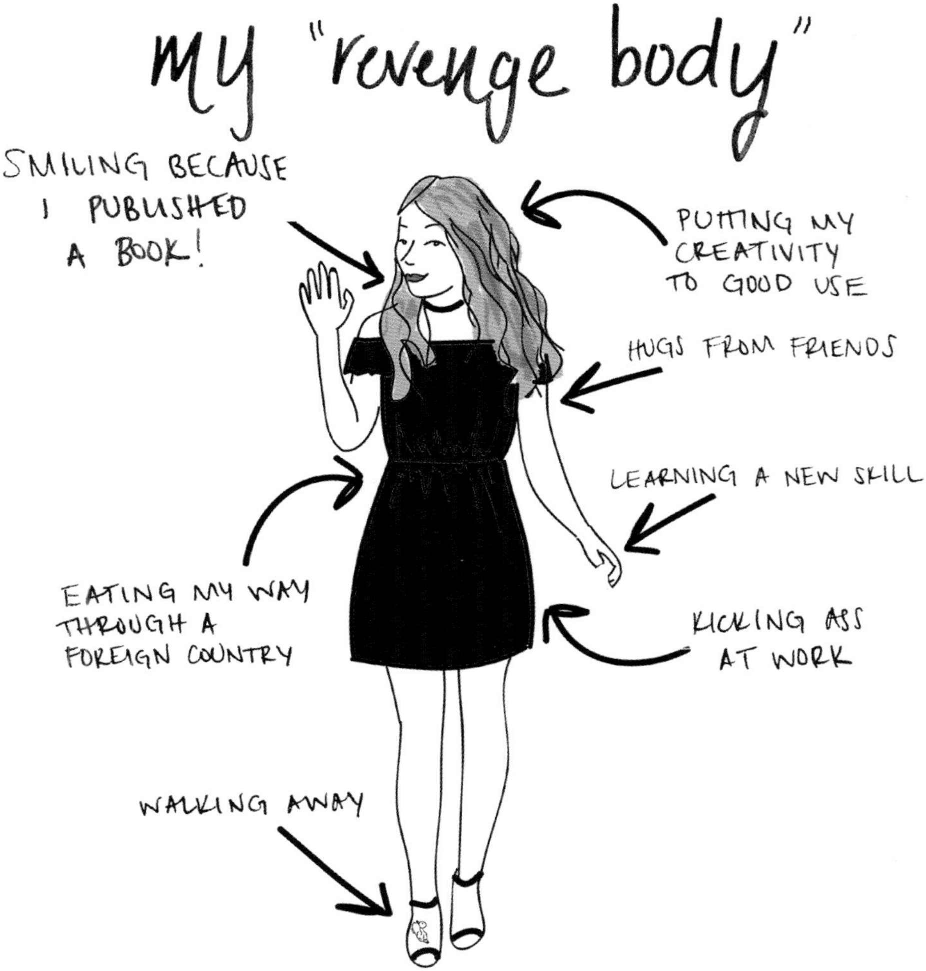
my "revenge body"
SMILING BECAUSE I PUBLISHED A BOOK!
PUTTING MY CREATIVITY TO GOOD USE
HUGS FROM FRIENDS
LEARNING A NEW SKILL
EATING MY WAY THROUGH A FOREIGN COUNTRY
KICKING ASS AT WORK
WALKING AWAY

the ultimate revenge is multifaceted
and more than skin deep.

you can't have flowers

without rain

and I still crave more flowers.

THOSE THINGS
I WAS
LONGING FOR

DON'T EXIST
ANYMORE

it won't ever go back to the way it was.

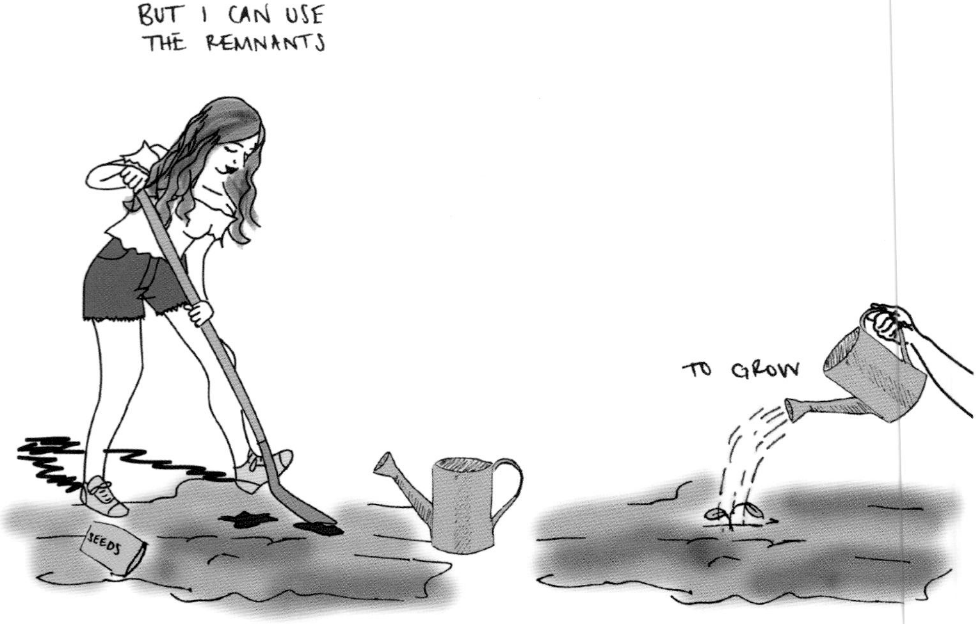
BUT I CAN USE
THE REMNANTS
SEEDS
TO GROW

something new, within me.

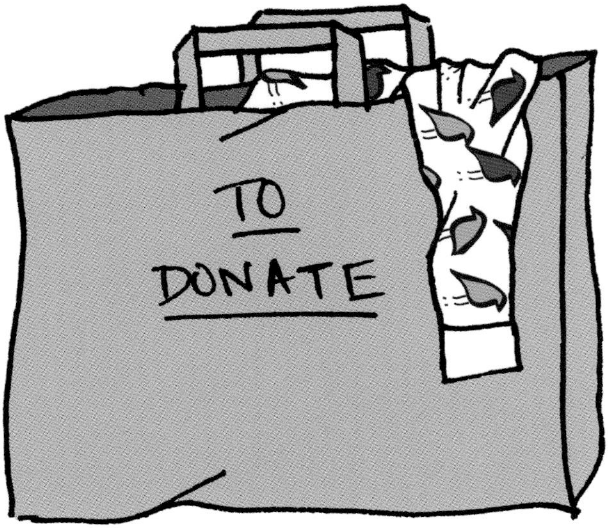
TO
DONATE

good riddance.

closure is...

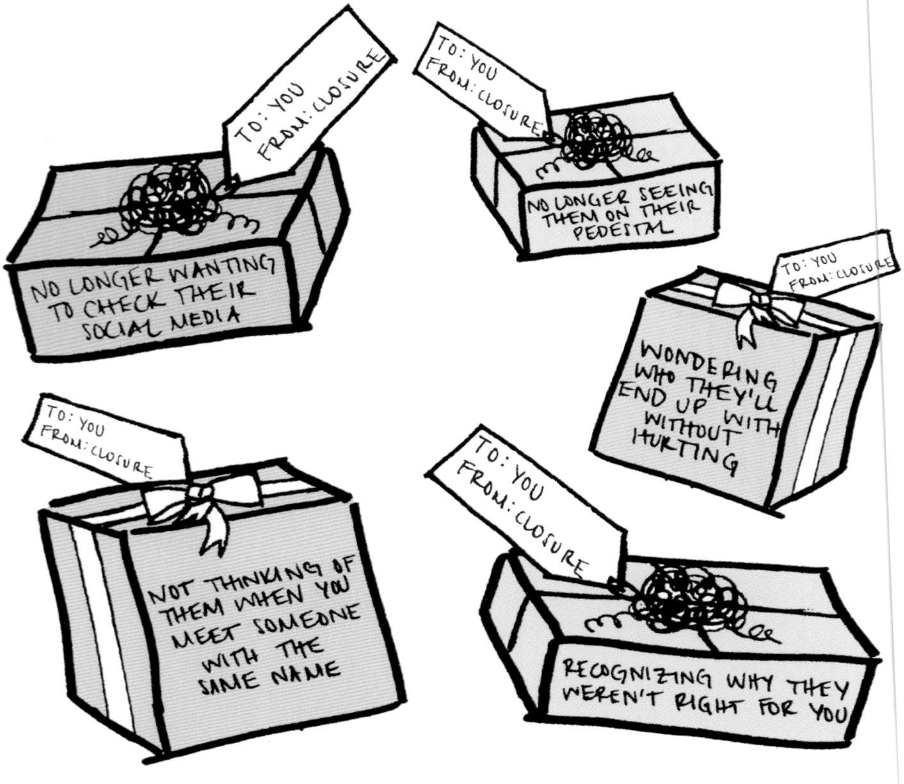
TO: YOU
FROM: CLOSURE
NO LONGER WANTING TO CHECK THEIR SOCIAL MEDIA
TO: YOU
FROM: CLOSURE
NO LONGER SEEING THEM ON THEIR PEDESTAL
TO: YOU
FROM: CLOSURE
WONDERING WHO THEY'LL END UP WITH WITHOUT HURTING
TO: YOU
FROM: CLOSURE
NOT THINKING OF THEM WHEN YOU MEET SOMEONE WITH THE SAME NAME
TO: YOU
FROM: CLOSURE
RECOGNIZING WHY THEY WEREN'T RIGHT FOR YOU

the best gifts I've ever received.

what does closure mean to you?

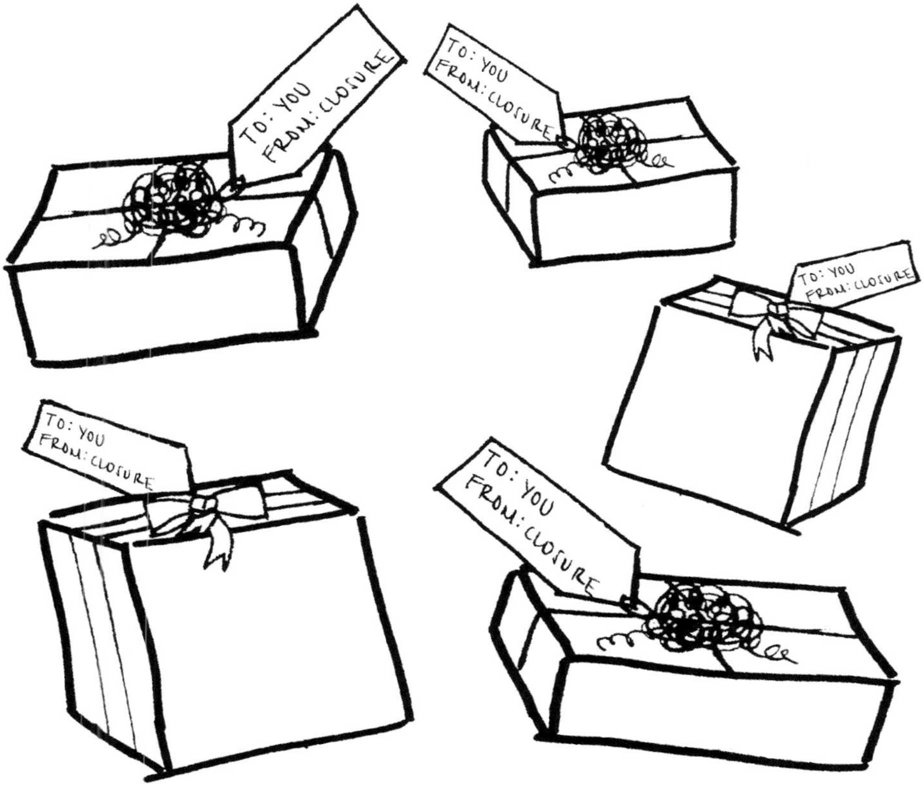
TO: YOU
FROM: CLOSURE
TO: YOU
FROM: CLOSURE
TO: YOU
FROM: CLOSURE
TO: YOU
FROM: CLOSURE
TO: YOU
FROM: CLOSURE

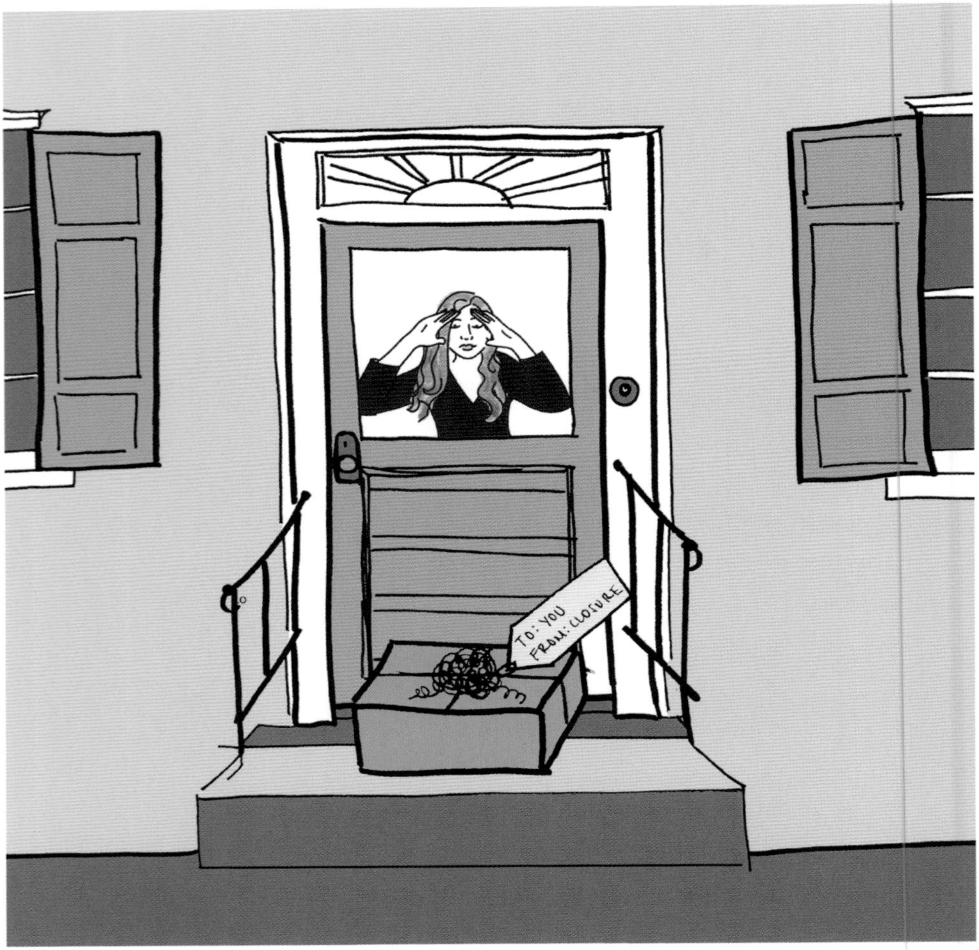
TO: YOU
FROM: CLOSURE

Amazon, is that you?

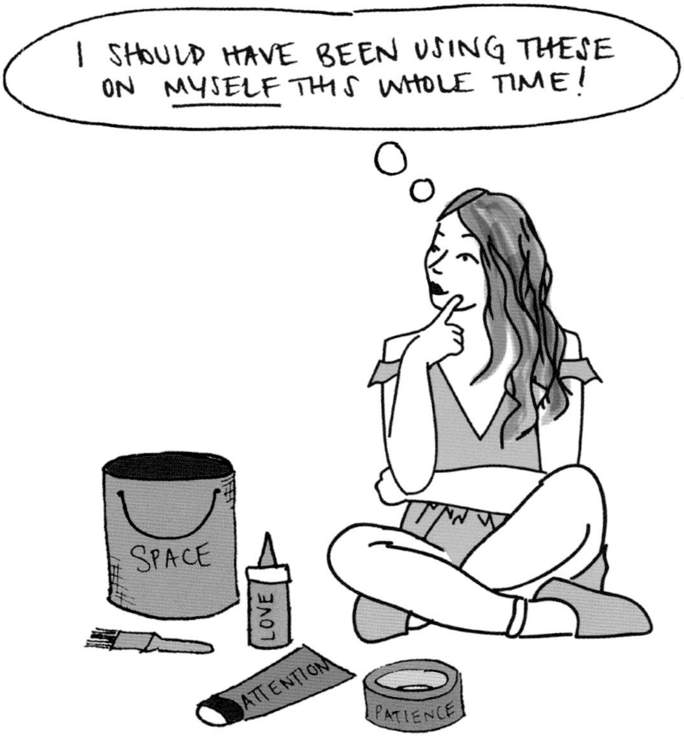
I SHOULD HAVE BEEN USING THESE ON MYSELF THIS WHOLE TIME!
SPACE
LOVE
ATTENTION
PATIENCE

they were wasted on you.

things you taught me about myself

I AM BLIND   ⟶   I AM SELF-AWARE

I AM CAPABLE OF PAIN ⟶ I AM CAPABLE OF LOVE

I AM ALLOWED TO ⟶ I AM ALLOWED TO
FEEL WEAK   FEEL STRONG

I CAN FEEL   ⟶   I CAN BE VERY
UNDESIRABLE   DESIRABLE

I CAN RECEDE   ⟶   I CAN EXPAND

I CAN BREAK   ⟶   I CAN REPAIR

perfectly imperfect.

what did you learn about yourself?

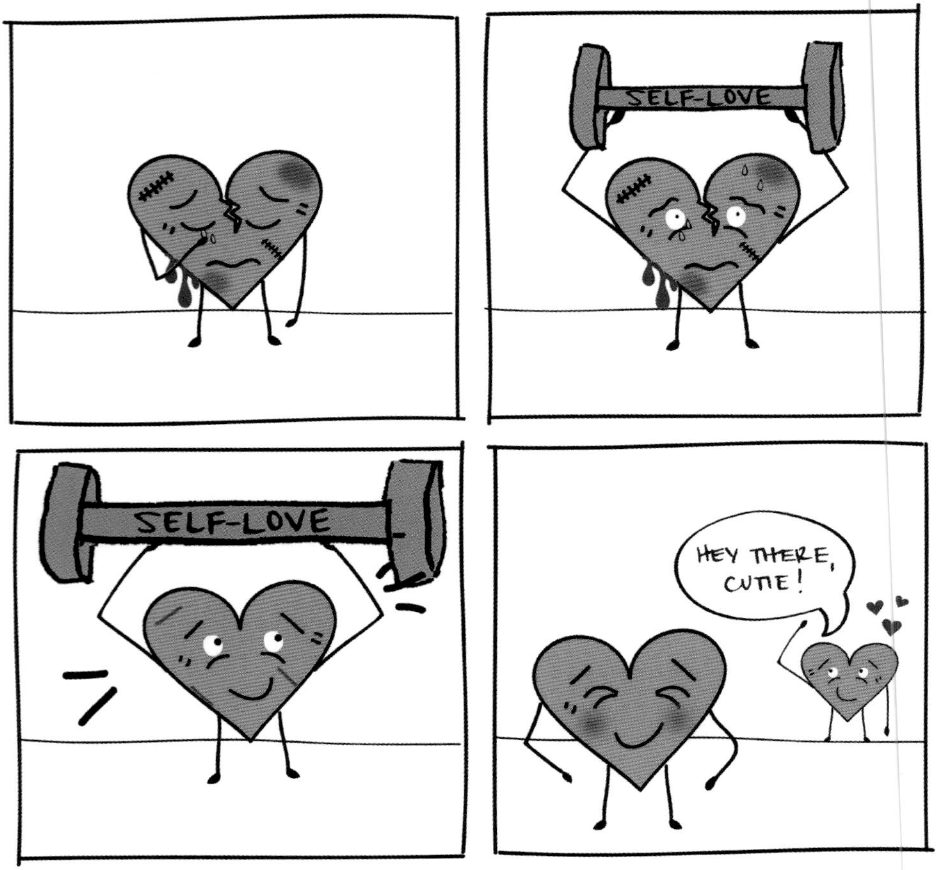
SELF-LOVE
SELF-LOVE
HEY THERE, CUTIE!

stronger than yesterday,
and everyone else is noticing.

things I will never apologize for

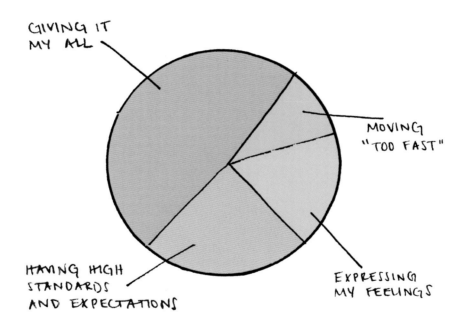

GIVING IT
MY ALL

MOVING
"TOO FAST"

HAVING HIGH
STANDARDS
AND EXPECTATIONS

EXPRESSING
MY FEELINGS

not sorry.

~~remind~~ reclaim

NEW YORK CITY

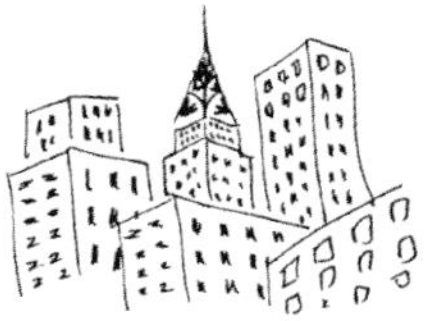

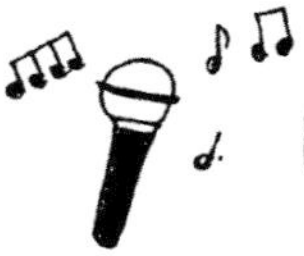

KARAOKE ON BIRTHDAYS

A CLICHÉ WE DISCOVERED WE BOTH SAY OFTEN

A PENNY FOR YOUR THOUGHTS

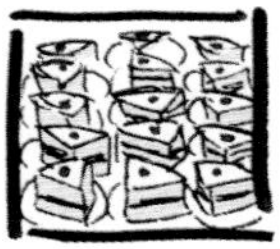

THE ARTIST WHOSE EXHIBIT WE SAW TOGETHER

THE PLAYLIST I MADE WHEN WE FIRST MET

happy mix

SHUFFLE PLAY

ILYSB
LANY · Make Out ...

Chocolate
The 1975 · The 1975 ...

Blinded
Third Eye Blind · Out... ...

BIRD SHIRTS

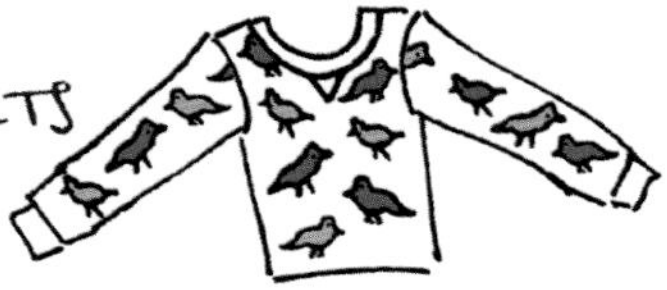

you're not fused with these anymore.

what will you reclaim?

you feel like

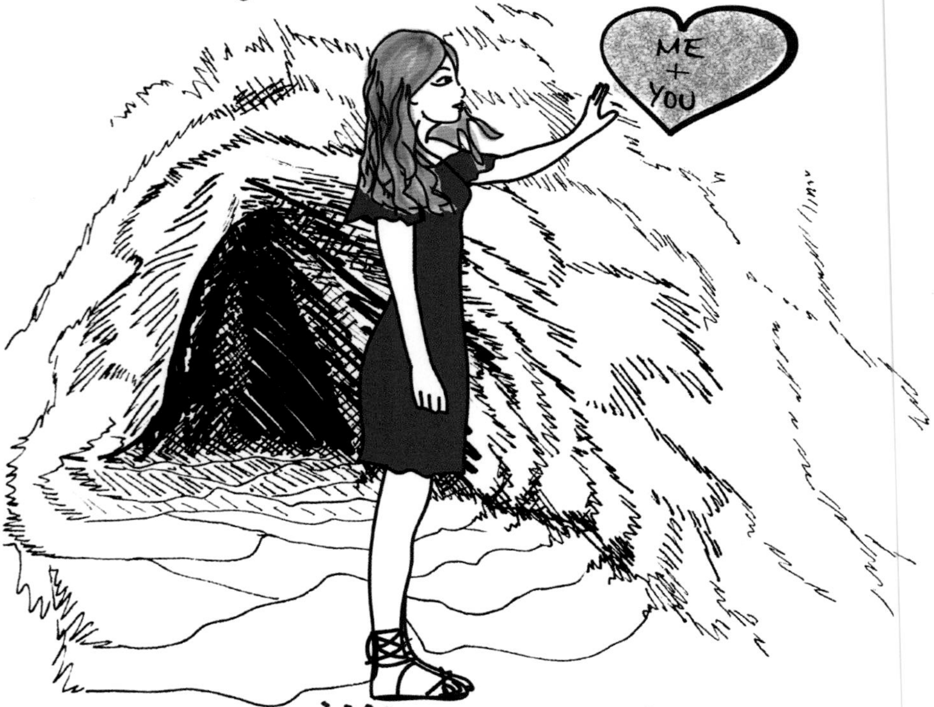
ME
+
YOU

a million years ago

an ancient part of my heart.

what makes me proud to be me

THE WAY I TREAT THE PERSON I LOVE ~~EVERYTHING I DID FOR MYSELF AFTER THEY LEFT~~

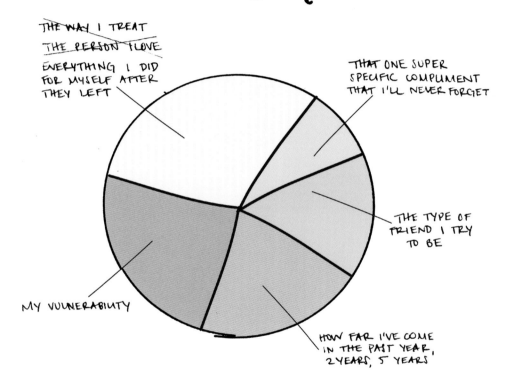

THE WAY I TREAT THE ~~PERSON I LOVE~~

EVERYTHING I DID FOR MYSELF AFTER THEY LEFT

THAT ONE SUPER SPECIFIC COMPLIMENT THAT I'LL NEVER FORGET

THE TYPE OF FRIEND I TRY TO BE

MY VULNERABILITY

HOW FAR I'VE COME IN THE PAST YEAR, 2 YEARS, 5 YEARS

resilience is the new black.

thank you

for giving me the
opportunity to make
myself even better
than I was before you

note to self.

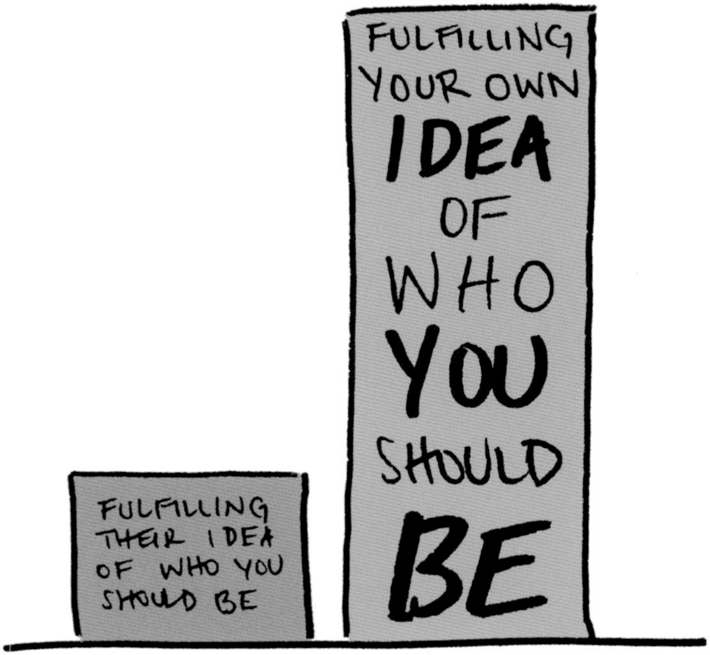
FULFILLING THEIR IDEA OF WHO YOU SHOULD BE
FULFILLING YOUR OWN IDEA OF WHO YOU SHOULD BE

a whole other level.

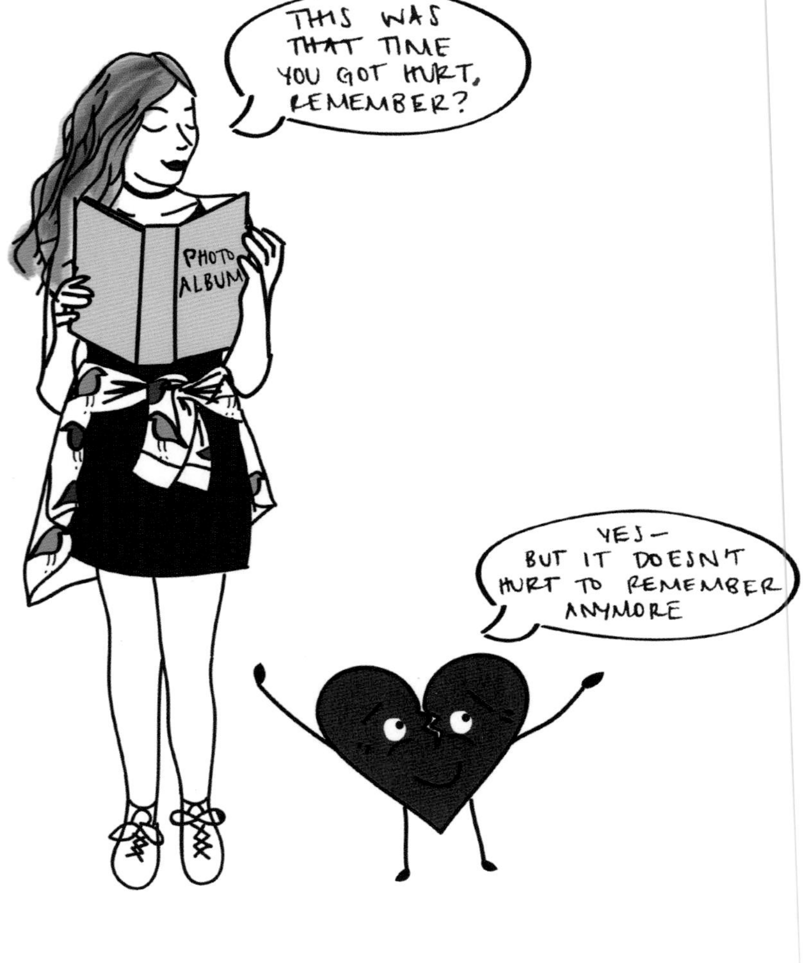
THIS WAS THAT TIME YOU GOT HURT, REMEMBER?
PHOTO ALBUM
YES— BUT IT DOESN'T HURT TO REMEMBER ANYMORE

I'll keep the good memories, though.

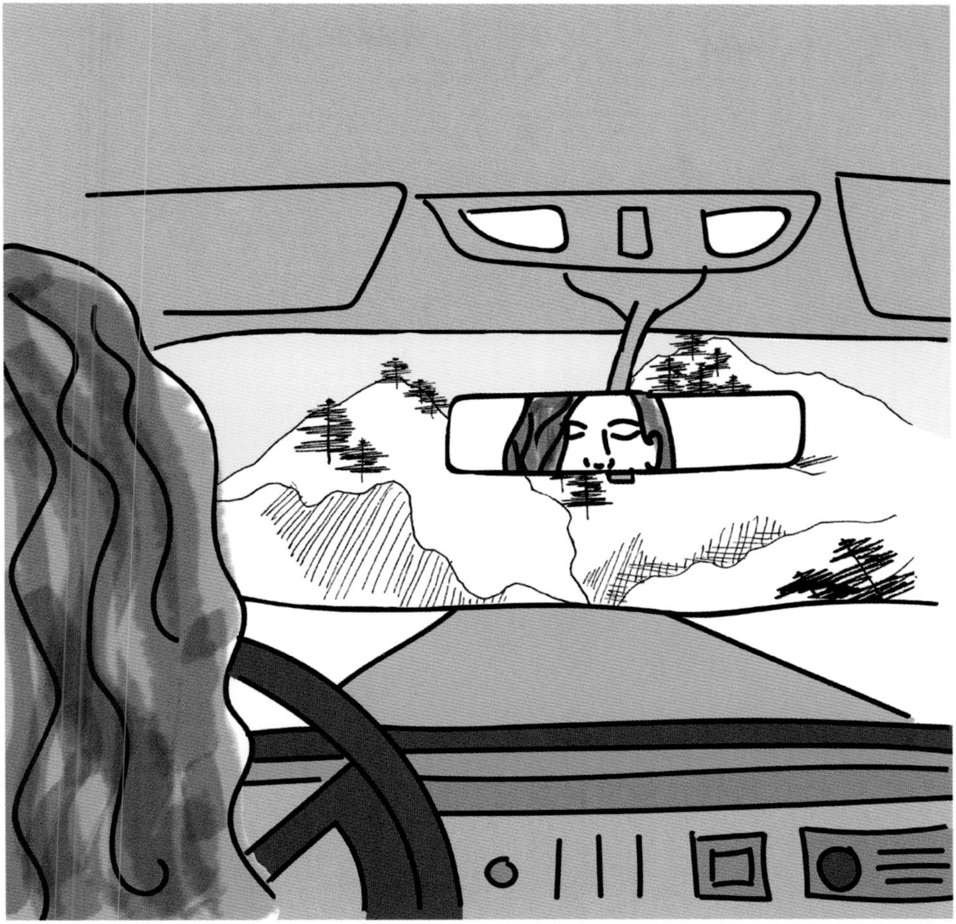

one last glance.

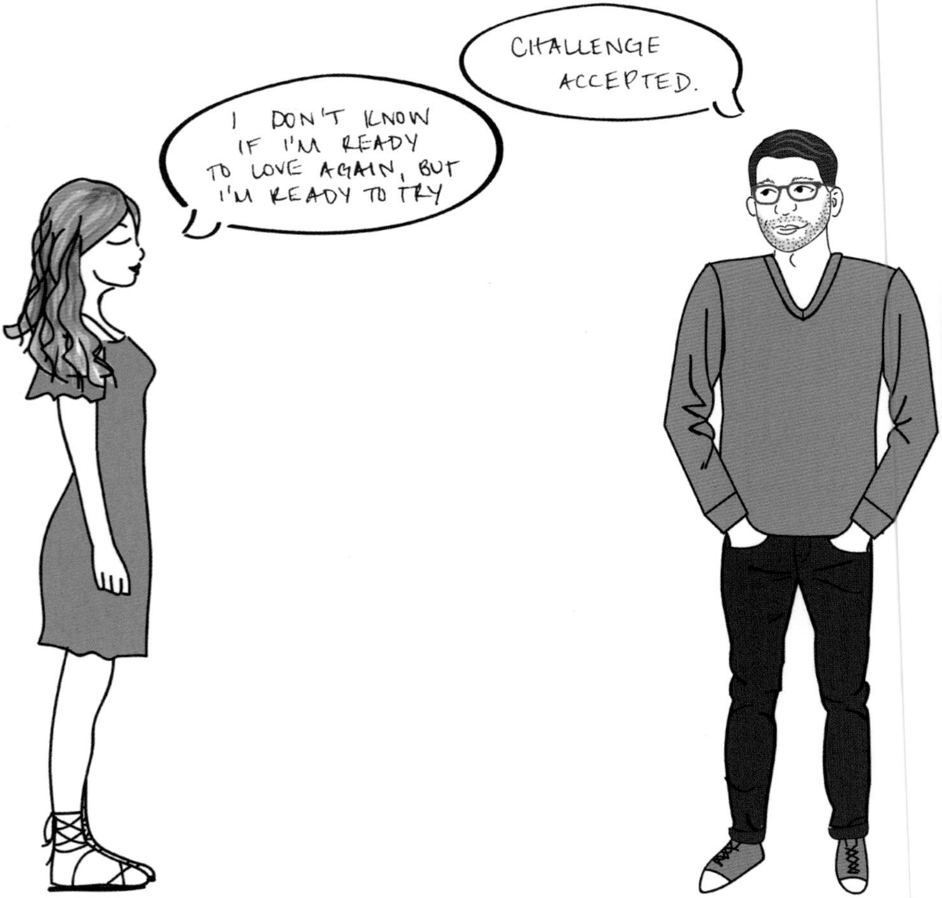
I DON'T KNOW IF I'M READY TO LOVE AGAIN, BUT I'M READY TO TRY
CHALLENGE ACCEPTED.

about the artist

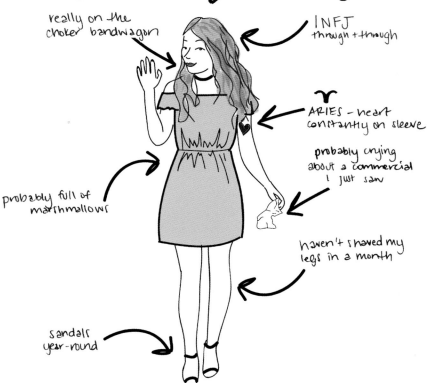

really on the
choker bandwagon

INFJ
through + through

ARIES - heart
constantly on sleeve

probably crying
about a commercial
I just saw

probably full of
marshmallows

haven't shaved my
legs in a month

sandals
year-round